FAITH ALONE

THE CONDITION OF OUR SALVATION

An Exposition of the Book of Galatians
and Other Relevant Topics

Other Books by Dr. Arnold G. Fruchtenbaum

Jesus Was a Jew

A Passover Haggadah for Jewish Believers

Ha-Mashiach: The Messiah of the Hebrew Scriptures

Biblical Lovemaking: A Study of the Song of Solomon

The Remnant of Israel:
The History, Theology, and Philosophy of the Messianic Jewish
Community

The Footsteps of the Messiah:
A Study of the Sequence of Prophetic Events

Israelology: The Missing Link in Systematic Theology

An Historical and Geographical Study Guide of Israel:
With a Supplement on Jordan

The Sabbath

God's Will & Man's Will:
Predestination, Election, and Free Will

Ariel's Bible Commentary Series:

The Messianic Jewish Epistles

Judges and Ruth

The Book of Genesis

FAITH ALONE

THE CONDITION OF OUR SALVATION

**An Exposition of the Book of Galatians
and Other Relevant Topics**

ARNOLD G. FRUCHTENBAUM
TH.M., PH.D.

MINISTRIES

ISBN 978-1-935174-45-5

Library of Congress Control Number: 2014952858

REL101000 RELIGION / Messianic Judaism

All Scripture quotations, unless otherwise noted, are from the *1901 American Standard Version* (Oak Harbor, WA: Logos Research Systems, Inc., 1994). However, the archaic language has been changed with one exception: The archaic *ye* has been retained in order to distinguish the second person plural from the singular *you*. The words *Jesus* and *Christ* have been replaced with *Yeshua* and *Messiah*.

Cover illustration by Jesse Gonzales (*http://www.vipgraphics.net*)

Editor: Christiane Jurik
Copy editors: Pauline Ilsen and Julie Petersen

Printed in the United States of America

Published by Ariel Ministries
P.O. Box 792507
San Antonio, TX 78279-2507
www.ariel.org

This volume is dedicated to

MOTTEL BALESTON

A great Bible teacher

Who fully understands God's program of salvation

By grace through faith

To the Jew first and also to the Greek.

Contents

Chapter I – The Problem

Exactly what must one do to be saved? For Bible-believing followers of Messiah, the answer should be easy. Whatever Scripture tells us are the elements that lead to salvation we will follow and adhere to. If only it were that simple!

Too many believers think they can and need to add to their salvation. By grace through faith alone does not seem to satisfy. People add the keeping of some of the laws of Moses to their salvation. Others believe their baptism plays a role in it. Again others throw what is commonly known as Lordship salvation into the mix. Especially within the messianic movement, elements like keeping *Torah*, adhering to Jewish customs, and observing biblical and traditional feasts tend to make favorite additions to salvation. A look at history shows that this has not always been the case.

The modern messianic movement is essentially a revival of the messianic movement that was present in the Land of Israel up until the end of the fourth century. While over the course of the next 1,400 years there have always been Jewish people who came to believe in the Messiahship of *Yeshua* (Jesus), they were generally forced to assimilate into the larger church and follow a policy of losing their Jewishness. The revival of the messianic movement more similar to the early church continues to adhere to the fact that *Yeshua* is the Messiah of Israel. At the same time, it also affirms the right of Messianic Jews to identify as Jews and maintain a

Jewish lifestyle, though the degree of practice may vary within different circles.

The roots of the modern movement formed in the eastern parts of Europe in the early 1800s. Unfortunately, the Holocaust decimated the Messianic Jewish population of Europe, so that, after the war, only a small percentage was left and without a united voice. In the 1970s, the modern Messianic Jewish movement was revived in the west, particularly in North America. Messianic Jewish congregations were established in various cities which provided Messianic Jews with an environment to maintain their Jewish lifestyle and identity.

Today, the movement has spread to all parts of the world where the larger Jewish community exists. I am a part of this movement, and the ministry I work with, Ariel Ministries, has planted several messianic congregations. Nevertheless, the movement is still undergoing many labor pains and growth pains, and it has not always been stable theologically. For a time, the majority of Messianic Jews was dispensational, but that is no longer true. The sad fact is that most Messianic Jews today are not well taught in Scripture and are part of fellowships that tend to be more experience oriented than Bible oriented. Generally, when the Scriptures are not expounded upon, there is less dispensational teaching.

This is not to say that most Messianic Jews follow Covenant Theology, because that doctrine by its very nature is Replacement Theology, and probably ninety-nine percent of all Messianic Jews reject Covenant Theology out of hand. So while most of them are not dispensational anymore in the broadest sense, they are dispensational in that they certainly believe in God's plan for the future of Israel. The non-dispensational aspects that permeate many messianic congregations pertain to two things: the teaching that messianic believers are still under the law and the rejection of Pretribulationalism, which is a tenet of Dispensationalism. However, the doctrine of a pretribulational Rapture is not limited to Dispensationalists since other groups, such as the Bible Presbyterian denomination, also hold to it.

Because of these inconsistencies in teaching, various branches within the messianic movement have sprung up. One of them is called the

Ephraimite or Two House movement. The followers of this theology falsely claim that Gentiles who come to believe are members of the lost tribes of Israel and therefore obligated to keep the *Torah*. Actually, this is nothing more than a repetition of the old Galatian heresy in which Jews who claimed to believe in *Yeshua* were telling Gentiles they had to submit to the Mosaic Law. If it were true that Gentiles who believe *in Yeshua* are really members of the lost sheep of the house of Israel, then why did Paul not tell the Galatians that they were really Israel and not Gentiles? Why did he tell them they should not submit to circumcision and the Mosaic Law?

If there was a really good time for New Testament writers to make clear that Gentile believers are members of lost Israel, Romans 11 would have been an ideal passage. Yet, throughout that passage, as well as in the preceding two chapters, Paul keeps referring to Gentile believers only as Gentiles. Not once does he imply they are really lost Israel. The very fact that Gentile believers are always referred to as Gentiles throughout the New Testament shows the fallacy of the view.

Another recent problem is the denial of the Triune nature of the God of Israel and, in turn, of the deity of the Messiah. Right now, only a small minority denies the Trinity, but the number has been growing.

Theories and heresies like the Ephraimite Theology spring up on a regular basis within Christendom and the messianic movement. In this book, then, we will be looking at the biblical conditions of salvation. We will be studying the Book of Galatians extensively to find out how the Apostle Paul dealt with people who tried to add the keeping of the *Torah* to salvation. We will be looking at how the Law of Moses really relates to the Law of Messiah. And we will discuss some of the false teachings that have been added to the biblical doctrine of salvation.

Chapter II –
The Correct Condition of Salvation

According to Scripture, salvation is based solely on faith in *Yeshua* the Messiah. Salvation is by grace through faith, and faith is the only condition for salvation. This is the starting point from which one must tackle the question what one must do to be saved.

In more than two hundred cases where the Scriptures give a condition for salvation, faith or belief is the one and only condition. This is important to remember. If there are "problem passages," one should not interpret the two hundred clear passages by the few minor problem passages. Rather, one should try to interpret the few problem passages by the two hundred clear passages. We shall do this in chapter V, which discusses false additions to salvation.

One of the clear passages is John 1:12:

> *But as many as received him, to them gave he the right to become children of God, even to them that believe on his name:*

This verse states that the ones who became the *children of God* are those who *received him*. What does it mean to receive the Messiah? The second part of the verse explains that to receive the Messiah means to *believe on his name*, to believe that He really is the Jewish Messiah. Simply by believing, one receives salvation. That is the way one becomes a child of God, and believing is the only condition mentioned here.

Another example is Acts 16:30-31:

³⁰and brought them out and said, Sirs, what must I do to be saved? ³¹And they said, Believe on the Lord Yeshua, and you shall be saved, you and your house.

In verse 30, the question is asked: *what* [exactly] *must I do to be saved?* When the apostles answer in verse 31, the only condition is to believe *on the Lord Yeshua*. If they believe *on the Lord Yeshua*, then they receive salvation.

These are just two of over two hundred examples where a condition is given for salvation, and the only condition spelled out is that of faith and belief. Because in the majority of cases that is the only condition given, one must be careful before assuming the Bible teaches there are additional conditions to salvation.

What is the content of a faith that saves? Faith that saves must be placed in the Messiah as our substitute for the penalty of our sin and as our Savior from the penalty of sin. Salvation is not merely believing that *Yeshua* existed. Some of the most pagan atheists believe that a man named *Yeshua* of Nazareth existed. Merely believing that *Yeshua* existed, merely believing that He died on the cross, and merely believing that He rose again from the dead does not save anyone. Rather, the believer's faith must be placed in the Messiah as his substitute for and as his Savior from the penalty of sin.

In other words, one needs to trust the Messiah for one's salvation. One must believe that He has accomplished the salvation work on one's behalf. To be saved, one must believe not just that He died, but that He died for one's own sins. If one believes that *Yeshua* the Messiah died for his sins, it presupposes that the person has confessed he is a sinner. If *Yeshua* died for our sins, obviously it means that we are sinners. So we must believe that *Yeshua* died for our sins as our substitute, that He was buried and rose again, and that He therefore has provided salvation. Thus, one trusts *Yeshua* for one's salvation.

> ### This is the condition of salvation:
>
> *Faith must be placed in the Messiah*
> *as one's substitute for and*
> *as one's Savior from*
> *the penalty of sin.*

In the context of the conditions of our salvation, the Scriptures use three Greek words.

The first term is **pistis**, which is used 243 times in the New Testament. It always has the meaning of "faith," with only four exceptions: Acts 17:31, where it has the meaning of *assurance*; II Thessalonians 2:13, where it is translated as *belief*; Titus 2:10, where it has the meaning of *fidelity*; and Hebrews 10:39, where it is translated *belief*, although some translations have *faith*. Except for these four occasions, the word *pistis* always has the meaning of "faith."

The second key Greek word is **pisteuo**, which is used a total of 246 times in the Greek New Testament. It always has the meaning "to believe," except for nine times: once it is translated as *believers* (Acts 5:14); and eight times it is translated as either *commit, committed*, or *intrusted* (Lk. 16:11; Jn. 2:24; Rom. 3:2; I Cor. 9:17; Gal. 2:7; I Thes. 2:4; Titus 1:3; I Tim. 1:11).

The third main Greek word is **peitho**, which means "to cause belief in a thing." This word is used fifty times in the Greek New Testament, and it is translated in nine different ways. It is translated as *persuade* twenty-two times; as *trust* ten times; as *confidence* nine times; as *obey* seven times; as *believed* three times; as *assure* one time; as *yield* once; as *made free* once; and as *access* once. But in spite of these nine different translations, the root meaning of the word remains the same: "to cause belief in a thing."

By combining these three Greek words, one can clearly determine what the condition of salvation is in reference to faith. To have faith means "to believe." It means "to be persuaded of." It means "to place confidence in." And it means "to trust in the sense of relying upon."

These are the four facets of faith when one places his trust in *Yeshua* the Messiah.

When the Scriptures speak of faith, they use the word in five senses:

1. Faith is used as "conviction that something is true."
2. Faith is used as "trust."
3. Faith is used as "persuaded," and it is stronger than mere opinion, though it is weaker than foreknowledge.
4. Faith is used as "belief based upon the facts of knowledge" (Rom. 10:14).
5. Faith must have an object. The object of faith is God, while the content of faith is the death of the Messiah for one's sins, His burial, and resurrection.

To conclude the first part of this study: the only condition of salvation is believing that the Messiah died for one's sins, was buried, and rose again, and trusting Him for one's salvation.

Chapter III –
The Book of Galatians

The problem that Paul was dealing with in his epistle to the Galatians concerns a group that has come to be known as "the Judaizers." These people felt that the Gentiles must obey the Law of Moses in order to be saved (Acts 15:1 and 5), and they continually followed Paul around. After the apostle left a city, they would come in with their false teachings. They did not have the sanction of the Jerusalem Church, and the Jerusalem Council of Acts 15:12-21 renounced their statements, beliefs, and teachings. Yet the Judaizers persisted in troubling Paul, and they were troubling these Galatians.

Because of their teaching that one must obey the Law of Moses in order to be saved, the ultimate issue in the book is: What is the gospel? What is the content of the gospel? Or, what must I do to be saved?

Unlike other epistles, Paul did not write the Book of Galatians to one particular church, but to several churches in the province of Galatia that contained the cities of Antioch of Pisidia, Iconium, Lystra, Derbe, and others. The apostle founded these churches on his first missionary journey (Acts 13:1—14:28). He went there again during his second missionary journey (Acts 15:36—18:22) as well as his third missionary journey (Acts 18:23—20:38).

Paul wrote this epistle for three reasons: First, to defend his apostolic authority, because Paul's claims to apostolic authority had been attacked by these Judaizers; second, to show that salvation is by grace through faith alone, which counteracts the teachings of the Judaizers; and third, to strengthen the faith of the believers in Galatia. Because it answers a lot of the questions addressed in this book, we will take the time to thoroughly study Paul's method of reasoning and his logic.

A. THE GREETING: GALATIANS 1:1-5

[1]Paul, an apostle (not from men, neither through man, but through Yeshua Messiah, and God the Father, who raised him from the dead), [2]and all the brethren that are with me, unto the churches of Galatia: [3]Grace to you and peace from God the Father, and our Lord Yeshua Messiah, [4]who gave himself for our sins, that he might deliver us out of this present evil world, according to the will of our God and Father: [5]to whom be the glory for ever and ever. Amen.

Paul began the letter quite normally. The pattern for an ancient letter was: "From A," "to B," "Greeting." Following that pattern, he writes, "From Paul to the churches of Galatia: Greeting." The "from" is: *Paul . . . and all the brethren* who are with him, according to verses 1-2a. The "to" is found in verse 2b: *the churches of Galatia.*

The Book of Galatians was an encyclical letter, meaning one to be circulated among the various churches in the province of Galatia. In his extended greeting, Paul brought out the three issues he wanted to deal with.

The first issue is the fact of his apostolic authority in verse 1: *Paul, an apostle.* Furthermore, his apostolic authority is *not from men, neither through man.* It is not *from* men in that his apostolic authority is not of human origin; nor is it *through man,* it did not come to him by any human instrumentality. His apostolic authority is of divine origin. It is *through Yeshua Messiah and God the Father,* through *Yeshua* the Messiah as the instrument and through God the Father as the source. So the ultimate

10

source of Paul's apostolic authority was God the Father, and his apostolic calling came by means of *Yeshua* the Messiah.

The second issue is that salvation is by grace through faith alone, according to verse 4a. Paul states that *Yeshua* the Messiah *gave himself for our sins*. This is the gospel: that *Yeshua* died for our sins, and the essence of the gospel carries the concept of substitution. The acceptance of the Messiah's substitutionary death is what saves, and that alone. The word *grace* is the key word throughout the letter and emphasizes that salvation is by grace through faith, plus nothing.

The third issue of this letter is to strengthen the faith of the Galatian believers by pointing out their sanctification in verses 4b-5. *Yeshua* came to save them out of the world; that is, out of this present evil age. This is the byproduct of grace: *that he might deliver us out of this present evil world, according to the will of our God and Father*. The will of God is the source of grace, and the glory of God is the reason and the goal of grace. Having mentioned God, he concludes with the word *Amen*.

B. THE PROBLEM: GALATIANS 1:6-10

[6]I marvel that ye are so quickly removing from him that called you in the grace of Messiah unto a different gospel; [7]which is not another gospel: only there are some that trouble you, and would pervert the gospel of Messiah. [8]But though we, or an angel from heaven, should preach unto you any gospel other than that which we preached unto you, let him be anathema. [9]As we have said before, so say I now again, If any man preaches unto you any gospel other than that which ye received, let him be anathema. [10]For am I now seeking the favor of men, or of God? or am I striving to please men? if I were still pleasing men, I should not be a servant of Messiah.

11

1. The Perversion of the Gospel – 1:6-7

In verse six, Paul begins by rebuking their fickleness, and he marvels at how quickly they have removed themselves from the teachings of *the grace of Messiah*. He is also surprised at the content, because what they have been deceived by is a *different gospel*.

In verse seven, he says that this new gospel is *not another gospel* but a perversion of the true gospel. There are two Greek words that mean "another." One term means "another of the same kind," and the second term means "another of a different kind." The Greek word Paul used here means "another gospel of a different kind." In other words, they were not receiving another gospel of the same kind, a similar gospel, but they were deceived by another gospel of a different kind, a gospel totally different from the one they had believed earlier. This is a different gospel than the gospel of grace. This is not even another gospel of the same kind, but it is another gospel of a different kind.

The Greek word for *pervert* means "to twist something around," "to reverse it." It means that they are not denying it; rather, they are destroying it by adding to it. They are taking true things and destroying them.

Throughout the letter, these perversions are seen in at least four areas. First, they believe in the perfection *in the flesh* (Gal. 3:3). Second, they believe in the obligatory observance of *days, and months, and seasons, and years* (Gal. 4:10). Third, they believe in being *justified by the law* (Gal. 5:4). And fourth, they believe in mandatory circumcision (Gal. 5:2). So, by these things the gospel was being perverted.

2. The Rebuke of False Teachers – 1:8-9

In verses 8-9, Paul pronounces the *anathema*, which is a rebuke against false teachers. Anyone who teaches a gospel that is different from the gospel they have received is to be *anathema*. Another gospel is any gospel other than the gospel of the grace of God. Any addition to the simple statement that salvation is by grace through faith is another gospel. Any addition to the gospel—be it baptism, tongues, ceremonies, church membership, repentance— perverts the gospel and is *anathema*.

The word *anathema* comes from the Hebrew concept of the *cherem*, which means "something that is untouchable," "something that is to be devoted to destruction." Anyone teaching a different gospel is to be devoted to destruction.

3. The Position of Paul – 1:10

In verse ten, Paul responds to his critics who claim that he is out to get converts by any means: to win the Jews, he keeps the law; to win the Gentiles, he sets the law aside. While it is true that Paul did keep the law, what he did not do was to make the keeping of the law obligatory, neither for salvation nor for sanctification. The same is true when Jewish believers today keep aspects of the law. While many of them claim it is obligatory, most do not. This is not the same as the Galatian heresy, because most Jewish believers today who observe Jewish customs do it on the basis of voluntary observance, not on the basis of obligatory observance. As long as it is merely voluntary, it is not a false addition to the gospel. If it becomes obligatory, then we have gone beyond the Scriptures.

The problem faced by the churches of Galatia was that they had received the doctrine of false teachers who claimed that merely believing on *Yeshua* is not enough to be saved. There is more involved. The "more" was the keeping of the law and the submission to the law by means of circumcision.

C. THE MAJOR ARGUMENTS: GALATIANS 1:11-6:10

After stating the problem, Paul then proceeds to the three major arguments of his book as he shows that salvation is by grace through faith plus nothing. The three major arguments Paul presents are biographical, theological, and practical.

1. The Biographical Argument – 1:11-2:21

In the first major argument, which is found in Galatians 1:11—2:21, Paul makes the point that he received independent revelation in five areas.

a. Independent of Human Teaching – 1:11-17

Paul begins by pointing out that his revelation was independent of human teaching in verses 11-12:

> *¹¹For I make known to you, brethren, as touching the gospel which was preached by me, that it is not after man. ¹²For neither did I receive it from man, nor was I taught it, but it came to me through revelation of Messiah Yeshua.*

The gospel that Paul preached did not come from any human source. The Judaizers claimed that Paul actually received his teachings from the apostles, so how dare he challenge teachers like the Judaizers who were coming from Jerusalem! Paul stated that his teachings did not come *after man* in that no man could frame this gospel.

The gospel is that salvation is by grace through faith plus nothing. Every human religion teaches salvation by works. Faith might be involved, but there is always the addition of works as part of the salvation package. Every human, man-made religion requires works for salvation. Even within Christendom, people have a hard time accepting the truth that salvation is by grace through faith plus nothing and begin to add things like baptism or church membership; they add elements and then claim that it is the "full gospel," implying that grace through faith alone is only a "partial gospel." The human tendency in formulating religion is that they want to add works to salvation.

Paul goes on to say that he did not receive the gospel from *man*. No human being taught these truths to Paul; he received them by divine *revelation* from *Yeshua* the Messiah. The word *revelation* means "making truth known that was previously unknown." Revelation is God's self-disclosure, and Paul received the things he was teaching during his three years of personal training by *Yeshua* in Arabia.

Furthermore, in verses 13 to 14, he points out that nothing in his previous life predisposed him to the gospel:

> *13For ye have heard of my manner of life in time past in the Jews' religion, how that beyond measure I persecuted the church of God, and made havoc of it: 14and I advanced in the Jews' religion beyond many of mine own age among my countrymen, being more exceedingly zealous for the traditions of my fathers.*

In fact, he was against grace, as he says in verse 13: He *persecuted the church . . . and made havoc of it* (Acts 8:1-3; 26:9-11). The Greek word for *havoc* means "to ravage" and "to devastate" a city. In other words, he had no leaning toward the gospel.

Furthermore, in verse 14, he states that he was for the law and made major advances in Judaism. The noun form of *advanced* in Greek is "trailblazer." He was a trailblazer in Judaism; he blazed new trails in Judaism. He was a member of the more extreme branch of the Pharisees, and he outstripped his peers in his zealousness for *the traditions of* [the] *fathers*. Nothing in his past predisposed him to the gospel.

He then explains how he received both the gospel and the apostleship in verses 15-17:

> *15But when it was the good pleasure of God, who separated me, even from my mother's womb, and called me through his grace, 16to reveal his Son in me, that I might preach him among the Gentiles; straightway I conferred not with flesh and blood: 17neither went I up to Jerusalem to them that were apostles before me: but I went away into Arabia; and again I returned unto Damascus.*

In verse 15, Paul states that he was predestined to receive the gospel and the apostleship: God *called me through his grace*. His office of apostleship was already picked for him by God, and, at a certain point in history, he received salvation when he was saved by grace. God then gave him his ministry to *preach* [the gospel] *among the Gentiles.* When he did so, he did not confer with any Jewish believers at that point, according to verse 16. In verse 17, he states that, upon salvation, he did not go to Jerusalem to confer with the other apostles. The fact that his gospel was the same as that of all the other apostles was evidence of its divine origin because both groups got it from God. He did not go to Jerusalem, but he went to *Arabia* and then *returned unto Damascus. Arabia* here does not refer to modern Arabia but to the Roman province of Arabia.

The point he makes in these verses is that he did not get the gospel of grace from man, but from God.

b. Independent of the Judean Churches – 1:18-24

18Then after three years I went up to Jerusalem to visit Cephas, and tarried with him fifteen days. 19But other of the apostles saw I none, save James the Lord's brother. 20Now touching the things which I write unto you, behold, before God, I lie not. 21Then I came into the regions of Syria and Cilicia. 22And I was still unknown by face unto the churches of Judaea which were in Messiah: 23but they only heard say, He that once persecuted us now preaches the faith of which he once made havoc; 24and they glorified God in me.

In verse 18, Paul points out that he was already an apostle before he ever went to Jerusalem. He had been with the Lord in personal training for three years in Arabia before he returned to Jerusalem. When he finally did go to Jerusalem, he was there for *fifteen days* only, and he spent those *fifteen days* with the Apostle Peter. This shows two things. First, it was too short a time for him to have received all of his truths from Peter. Second, it was long enough to be exposed if his gospel was different than the gospel of the other apostles. The visit he made was purely for the purpose of getting acquainted.

Furthermore, he saw none of the other apostles at that point except *James*—not James the brother of John, but James the half-brother of *Yeshua* (verse 19).

In verse 20, Paul then reaffirmed the truth of what he is saying. After fifteen days, he left Judea and traveled to the provinces of *Syria and Cilicia*, recorded in verse 21.

For the most part, he was totally unknown among *the churches of Judea* according to verses 22-24. He was mostly unknown to the church in Jerusalem and totally unknown to the other Judean churches. He did not get his gospel from the Jerusalem Church, nor did he get his gospel and his teachings from the other Judean churches. He was independent of them.

c. *Independent of the Judaizers – 2:1-10*

In verses 1-3 of Galatians 2, Paul points out that he was independent of the Judaizing brethren:

> *¹Then after the space of fourteen years I went up again to Jerusalem with Barnabas, taking Titus also with me. ²And I went up by revelation; and I laid before them the gospel which I preach among the Gentiles but privately before them who were of repute, lest by any means I should be running, or had run, in vain. ³But not even Titus who was with me, being a Greek, was compelled to be circumcised:*

In verse 1, he first states that he returned to Jerusalem only after *fourteen years* had transpired; between chapters 1 and 2, *fourteen years* had passed. The occasion for his return was the Jerusalem Council, spoken of in Acts 15:1-4. Paul states that he brought Titus with him. Titus was a Gentile believer who would serve as a test case. Titus was a prime example of a Gentile who was saved apart from the law and apart from circumcision. The very presence of Titus would be a challenge to the Judaizers. If Titus was required to be circumcised, then all Gentiles would be obligated to be circumcised. The thing to note is that the issue here is not circumcision for Jewish believers, but circumcision for Gentile believers. The issue of circumcision for the Jewish believer is in a different category than what is happening right here.

In verses 2-3, Paul stated that he had a private council with the key leaders of the Jerusalem Church. He first presented the gospel he was teaching to the leaders just in case he might have been running in the wrong race. He did this to see if the other apostles would authenticate his gospel. The leaders of the Jerusalem Church did not require circumcision for Titus. This showed that they validated the gospel that Paul preached. Here again, the emphasis was upon his being a Gentile. Now Timothy, of course, was circumcised by Paul, in Acts 16:1-3, but he had Jewish origins, so his circumcision was not an inconsistency on Paul's part. The issue here was not Jewish circumcision, but Gentile circumcision.

After the private council, he had a public council, described in verses 4-5:

>*⁴and that because of the false brethren privily brought in, who came in privily to spy out our liberty which we have in Messiah Yeshua, that they might bring us into bondage: ⁵to whom we gave place in the way of subjection, no, not for an hour; that the truth of the gospel might continue with you.*

Here is where the *false brethren* were brought in, the same ones who were mentioned in Acts 15:5. These were not true believers, but they claimed to be believers. Paul says they were *privily brought in*, meaning they were "planted" by someone from the outside to *spy out* [their] *liberty*. The Greek word means "to make a treacherous investigation." It is a metaphor of spies sneaking into the enemy camp, playing the part of friends when, in reality, they are enemies who have come to discover weak points. The reason they were brought in was *to bring us into bondage*. The Greek word means "to enslave completely." At that point, Jewish evangelism and discipleship was still within Judaism, and the Pharisees were there to attempt to retain the law and so demand circumcision.

According to verse five, Paul made no concessions to the Judaizers or to the Pharisees. He reminded them that he fought for Gentile liberty that *the gospel might continue*, that salvation is by grace through faith plus nothing. He demonstrated that Gentiles were being saved apart from the law and apart from circumcision.

Paul then gives three results of that conference in verses 6-10:

⁶But from those who were reputed to be somewhat (whatsoever they were, it makes no matter to me: God accepts not man's person)—they, I say, who were of repute imparted nothing to me: ⁷but contrariwise, when they saw that I had been intrusted with the gospel of the uncircumcision, even as Peter with the gospel of the circumcision ⁸(for he that wrought for Peter unto the apostleship of the circumcision wrought for me also unto the Gentiles); ⁹and when they perceived the grace that was given unto me, James and Cephas and John, they who were reputed to be pillars, gave to me and Barnabas the right hands of fellowship, that we should go unto the Gentiles, and they unto the circumcision; ¹⁰only they would that we should remember the poor; which very thing I was also zealous to do.

The first result of the conference is found in verse six: Paul's message was viewed as being a complete, full gospel. Nothing new needed to be added. There was no fresh knowledge imparted to Paul, and they saw no defect in his preaching; he was treated as an equal.

Second, verses 7-8 laid down the principle of two missions: Jewish missions and Gentile missions. The apostles did come out for Paul's apostolic authority, and Paul and Peter were viewed as equals, though working in different areas. Peter was the apostle to the circumcision while Paul was the apostle to the uncircumcision.

Third, in verses 9-10, Paul and Barnabas were given *the right hands of fellowship*, as we also see in Acts 15:22-29. The ministry of Paul was authenticated by the three *pillars* of the Jerusalem Church: James, Peter, and John. They all treated him as an equal. In fact, in Acts 15:13-21 James was not only a defender of the Jewish believer's position, but also of the Gentile believer's position. The only admonition they gave to Paul was to *remember the poor*, the Jewish believers in Jerusalem who became poor because they carried the brunt of persecution, and this Paul was *zealous to do* anyway.

d. Independent of Apostolic Pressure – 2:11-18

The fourth point of Paul's biographical argument is that he was independent even of apostolic pressure.

(1) The Hypocrisy of Peter

In light of the fact that Peter, according to verses 1-10, stood with Paul at the Jerusalem Council, Paul begins this argument with an account of Peter's hypocrisy, in verses 11-13:

> *2:11But when Cephas came to Antioch, I resisted him to the face, because he stood condemned. 12For before that certain came from James, he ate with the Gentiles; but when they came, he drew back and separated himself, fearing them that were of the circumcision. 13And the rest of the Jews dissembled likewise with him; insomuch that even Barnabas was carried away with their dissimulation.*

The very fact that Peter was hypocritical shows that not even the apostles were always inspired. They were inspired when they wrote Scripture; they were inspired when they were speaking in the name of the Lord; but they were not always inspired on a day-by-day, hour-by-hour, moment-by-moment basis.

After leaving Jerusalem, Peter came to the Church of Antioch where Paul was working (verses 11-13). This was a mixed church of Jewish and Gentile believers. When he first came, Peter had no problem eating with the Gentiles. After all, he had already come into the house of a Gentile in Acts 10. But when Jewish believers from Jerusalem came, Peter withdrew from the Gentiles even though he sided with Paul in the Jerusalem Council (Acts 15:7-11). The basis for Peter's withdrawal was not conscience or conviction, but fear.

When Peter, the apostle of the circumcision, withdrew, the other Jewish believers of the Church of Antioch also withdrew from the Gentile believers, including Barnabas, who should have known better, so, in verse 13, a split was developing. It created a division in observing the

Lord's Supper, and now there were two communions: a Jewish communion and a Gentile communion. The presumption was that the Jews had something that the Gentiles did not have.

(2) The Rebuke of Peter

Seeing clearly the hypocrisy of it all, at that point Paul defended the position that was already authenticated in Jerusalem. He first spelled out the issue before Peter in verse 14:

> *2:14But when I saw that they walked not uprightly according to the truth of the gospel, I said unto Cephas before them all, If you, being a Jew, live as do the Gentiles, and not as do the Jews, how compel you the Gentiles to live as do the Jews?*

He pointed out that Peter was guilty of walking *not uprightly*. The Greek word means, "to deviate from a straight course." By his actions, Peter was showing that he expected Gentile believers to live as Jews. Before the people came from Jerusalem, he lived and ate with Gentiles, but now that they had come, he reverted back to living like a Pharisaic Jew.

Paul's question was: Should the Gentiles now live as Jews? What Paul was telling Peter is that he was asking the Gentiles to accept what Peter himself had already discarded.

(3) The Defense of Paul's Rebuke

After pointing out the issue of Peter's hypocrisy, he then defends his rebuke of Peter in two ways.

> *2:15We being Jews by nature, and not sinners of the Gentiles, 16yet knowing that a man is not justified by the works of the law but through faith in Yeshua Messiah, even we believed on Messiah Yeshua, that we might be justified by faith in Messiah, and not by the works of the law: because by the works of the law shall no flesh be justified.*

21

His first defense spells out the Jewish believer's position or situation. He states that both he and Peter were Jews by birth. They were not even Gentile proselytes to Judaism. They were not born as sinners among the Gentiles. Yet both Paul and Peter now realize that they could not be justified by the law, and the very fact that they trusted *Yeshua* for their salvation showed that there was something lacking in Judaism.

They realized that they had to be justified by faith, not *by the works of the law*. Paul tells Peter that even as Jews they saw the need for trusting in the Messiah to be saved, and they trusted Him to do for them what the law failed to do. Faith was the means of justification, not the law.

The conclusion is: "Peter, why ask Gentiles to accept what Jews themselves have now recognized as being unfulfilling?" Both Paul and Peter recognized this. His first defense is basically this: "We were born as Jews, and yet, as Jews we realized that we could not be justified by the works of the law, but only justified by faith."

His second defense, found in verses 17-18, is that there is a real danger to Christology.

> *2:17But if, while we sought to be justified in Messiah, we ourselves also were found sinners, is Messiah a minister of sin? God forbid. 18For if I build up again those things which I destroyed, I prove myself a transgressor.*

If they persist on moving in this way, there is danger in that they will make the Messiah *a minister of sin*. The law was not a basis for justification, according to verse 17. Paul again points out that "though we as Jews seek to be justified, we have found that we are justified by faith through the Messiah. In order for us to be justified by faith through the Messiah, we must forsake our attempts to be justified by the works of the law." Now, if forsaking the law is sin, then the Messiah is indeed *a minister of sin*. That is the danger to Christology. We must turn away from seeking to be justified by the law to turn in faith to the Messiah, but if the turning is sin, then the Messiah becomes *a minister of sin*.

According to verse 18, to go back to the law after being justified by the Messiah actually means to go back to sin. It is as simple as that. A similar point is made in I Corinthians 7:18-34.

In this action, Paul showed he was independent of even apostolic pressure and was willing to stand up to Peter.

e. Independent of Selfish Interest – 2:19-21

19For I through the law died unto the law, that I might live unto God. 20I have been crucified with Messiah; and it is no longer I that live, but Messiah lives in me: and that life which I now live in the flesh I live in faith, the faith which is in the Son of God, who loved me, and gave himself up for me. 21I do not make void the grace of God: for if righteousness is through the law, then Messiah died for nought.

In verse 19, Paul states that, upon salvation, he died through the law. He was dead through the law because the law kills. Through the law, one is convicted; through the law, one is punished. The law reveals sins, the law provokes sin, and the law condemns. But now he is dead to the law, because once one is killed through the law, he becomes dead to the law; the law no longer has any jurisdiction over him. Paul became dead to the law that he *might live unto God.* He was resurrected spiritually to a new law and a new life. The believer goes from one jurisdiction to another, from the law to the Messiah, from the old jurisdiction to a new one.

Then, in verse 20, Paul spells out the manner in which one dies to the law. The Messiah took our punishment on the cross, and, positionally, the believer was crucified with the Messiah (Rom. 6:1-14). By being co-crucified with the Messiah, he died through the law and is now dead to the law. Once crucified, the law no longer has any jurisdiction over him (Rom. 7:4-6). He now has a new life. He now lives under a new jurisdiction, under grace.

Finally, in verse 21, Pauls points out that if a man can save himself by keeping the law, then the death of the Messiah was useless. But grace is not annulled in this way. If the law could make a man righteous, then the Messiah died for nothing. But the law could not make anyone righteous.

2. The Theological Argument – 3:1-4:31

In the second major argument for a salvation that's based on faith alone, Paul shows the failure of legalism. In developing this argument, he makes seven points.

a. Personal Experience – 3:1-5

¹O foolish Galatians, who did bewitch you, before whose eyes Yeshua Messiah was openly set forth crucified? ²This only would I learn from you. Received ye the Spirit by the works of the law, or by the hearing of faith? ³Are ye so foolish? having begun in the Spirit, are ye now perfected in the flesh? ⁴Did ye suffer so many things in vain? if it be indeed in vain. ⁵He therefore that supplies to you the Spirit, and works miracles among you, does he it by the works of the law, or by the hearing of faith?

Paul begins the theological argument by showing the failure of legalism from personal experience. The point he makes is that the Galatians own personal experience should have taught them that God was working on the basis of faith, not on the basis of the works of the law. He teaches this by asking six rhetorical questions. The first question is merely a question of surprise, while questions two through six are questions in which he spells out the norm of the spiritual life. By means of these rhetorical questions, the apostle will force the Galatians to see the light from their own personal experience.

The first rhetorical question is in verse one: "Are you so foolish?" The word Paul uses is a word that denotes stupidity. "Are you really so stupid?" Then he asks, "Who bewitched you?" The Greek word for *bewitch* is used only here in the entire New Testament. It is a reference to the "evil eye," "the mysterious power of evil." Paul thus states that only witchcraft could have gotten them to think the way they are now thinking about the need to obey the law. He points out that the Messiah had been publicly *set forth*, publicly presented before them as *crucified*. The death of *Yeshua* is all-sufficient; they do not need to add any works of the law to the death of the Messiah.

The second rhetorical question is in verse two: "On what basis did you receive the Holy Spirit? Did you receive it on the basis of *the works of the law*? No! On the basis of *the hearing of faith*? Yes!" There is a clear superiority of faith over works. Paul also makes this point in Romans 10:13-17.

The third rhetorical question is in verse 3a: "You are not stupid, are you?" Yet, the way they are headed, the implication is: "Yes, you are stupid about doing something this foolish."

The fourth rhetorical question is in verse 3b: "Can you finish *in the flesh* what you have *begun in the Spirit?* The answer here is obviously "no." The fact that the sanctification process is begun by the Spirit and the fact that sanctification is completed by the Spirit shows that we are not sanctified by the works of the law. Earlier, he showed the superiority of faith over works. Now, he shows the superiority of Spirit over flesh. The Judaizers were teaching that, yes, one is justified by faith, but he is sanctified by the law. They did not discount the fact that one had to believe in *Yeshua*, but added that one is sanctified by the works of the law. That is exactly what this fourth question denies.

The fifth rhetorical question is in verse four: "You have suffered so much for your faith. Was it all for nothing since you cannot be saved until you are circumcised?" The thrust of the question is: "You did not suffer so many things for nothing, did you?" If up to now they are still unsaved because they have not yet been circumcised, it means they have suffered all those persecutions as believers for nothing.

The last rhetorical question is found in verse five: "On what basis did God give you the Spirit and the working of miracles? Was it on the basis of the law? No! By *the hearing of faith*? Yes."

The conclusion, then, is that their own personal experience should have told them that all they have received was on the basis of faith, not on the basis of works. Personal experience alone should have told them, and yet, they were too stupid to learn from it.

b. Old Testament Teaching – 3:6-14

Paul continues the theological argument by showing the failure of legalism from the teachings of the Old Testament.

(1) Abraham's Justification by Faith

Paul begins with the example of Abraham because the patriarch operated in the spirit of faith, not in the spirit of the law. Verse six states:

> *3:6 Even as Abraham believed God, and it was reckoned unto him for righteousness.*

Abraham was the father of the Jewish people, and he was justified by faith according to Genesis 15:6. The content of his faith was that God would give him a son (Gen. 15:1-5). He *believed* the promises of God; the promises of God were the content of Abraham's faith. That is why we call the period in which he lived the Dispensation of Promise: he had faith in the promises of God. That point is made again in Romans 4:18-22 and Hebrews 11:8-12. The spiritual experience of Abraham, which was on the basis of faith, is to become the pattern for the New Testament believer.

The true *sons of Abraham* are those who exercise the same faith, as it says in verse seven:

> *3:7 Know therefore that they that are of faith, the same are sons of Abraham.*

Those who take their stand on the same principle are *sons*, eligible for the same blessing. The word *sons* in Jewish thinking has the meaning of "followers." So the term *sons of Abraham* means "Abraham's followers." He is not teaching that Gentiles become "spiritual Jews." Rather, those who follow the pattern of Abraham and exercise faith are the true children of Abraham. By calling all believers the *sons of Abraham*, he does not call all believers "spiritual Jews." Jewishness is not determined by Abraham alone, but by Abraham, Isaac, and Jacob. It is interesting that Gentile believers are never referred to as "the sons of Jacob," only as the *sons of Abraham*. So by calling Gentile believers the *sons of Abraham*, Paul does not mean they are spiritual Jews, but rather they follow Abraham's pattern in that they go on the basis of faith, not on the basis of works. Those who are the *sons of Abraham* are not spiritual Jews, but simply followers of Abraham's pattern, because that is what the phrase "sons of" generally means in Hebrew; that is, "a follower of." Spiritual Jews are Jews who happen to believe and exercise faith. Gentiles who believe and exercise faith are spiritual Gentiles and are the spiritual seed of Abraham, but that does not make them spiritual Jews.

In verse eight, Paul then points out that this Gentile blessing had been foretold:

> *3:8 And the scripture, foreseeing that God would justify the Gentiles by faith, preached the gospel beforehand unto Abraham, saying, In you shall all the nations be blessed.*

All the way back in Abraham's day, it was already prophesied that the Gentiles would be justified *by faith*. Abraham received the good news about Isaac and about the Messiah. The gospel of good news to Abraham was that he would have a son. Abraham exercised faith in the promise of that son, Isaac. The gospel to the Gentiles was faith in the promise of the Son, the Messiah. The simple good news was that Abraham would have a son, and because he believed that, he was saved. As for the Gentiles, because they believed in the Son—the Son of God, the Messiah—they, too, are saved by faith. This is the way the Gentiles will be *blessed*.

Having used the example of Abraham, he now draws his summary conclusion in verse nine:

> *3:9 So then they that are of faith are blessed with the faithful Abraham.*

Gentiles who take their stand on faith are candidates for the blessings of Abraham. The key blessing of Abraham was salvation by grace through faith, apart from works.

(2) The Blessing of Justification

3:10For as many as are of the works of the law are under a curse: for it is written, Cursed is every one who continues not in all things that are written in the book of the law, to do them. 11Now that no man is justified by the law before God is evident: for, The righteous shall live by faith; 12and the law is not of faith; but, He that does them shall live in them.

Paul points out that those who operate in the sphere of faith receive the blessing of justification in these verses.

In verse ten, he begins by declaring that those who are under the law, those who operate in the sphere of the law, *are under a curse.* This is the converse of those operating in the sphere of faith. He quotes Deuteronomy 21:23, which teaches that *he that is hanged is accursed of God.* James 2:10 teaches that unless you keep the law perfectly—unless you keep every single commandment—you are in violation of the whole law. In fact, to break only one commandment is to incur the guilt of breaking the whole law. There is a special curse on those who do not follow and obey every precept, yet, apart from the Messiah, no one has ever kept it perfectly. All are under its curse, and the curse of the law means physical death. Therefore, those who operate in the sphere of the law *are under a curse.*

Furthermore, in verse 11, there is no justification *by the law.* The very fact that the Old Testament states that justification was by faith means that the Old Testament itself saw that there is no justification by the works of the law. Obedience cannot pay for sin.

Then, to prove that the law does not justify, he quotes Habakkuk 2:4, which indicates that even in the Old Testament, one was justified by faith, not by the works of the law.

Finally, in verse 12, Paul declares: *the law is not of faith,* so those who operate in the sphere of the law do not receive the blessings of faith (Lev. 18:5). Those who operate in the sphere of the law are under a curse, but those who operate in the sphere of faith live under a blessing.

> *Obedience cannot pay for sin.*

(3) The Work of Messiah and the Law

3:13 Messiah redeemed us from the curse of the law, having become a curse for us; for it is written, Cursed is every one that hangs on a tree: 14that upon the Gentiles might come the blessing of Abraham in Messiah Yeshua; that we might receive the promise of the Spirit through faith.

In verse 13, the key is the fact that the Messiah became *a curse for us*. The pronoun *us* refers to Jewish believers, because it was Jews, not Gentiles who were under the law. The Messiah became a curse for *us* Jewish believers. The word *for* in the Greek means "in our stead." He became a curse in our stead; He was the "representative" in our place; He took the penalty of the law and suffered a penal death. Gentiles who put themselves under the law, as these Galatian Gentiles were thinking of doing, would, in turn, place themselves under a curse from which the Messiah had already delivered the Jews. He then points out how the Messiah "became the curse." According to Deuteronomy 21:22-23, everyone that hangs upon a tree is under a curse, and this is the kind of death that *Yeshua* died. The failure to keep the law meant death. Upon death, there was the hanging upon the tree to show the point of the curse. Of course, the Messiah kept the law perfectly and had every right to live. However, He did die under the law, but His death was substitutionary, and He took the curse by hanging upon a tree. The Jewish believers were redeemed from *the curse of the law* in that way.

In verse 14, the results of the Messiah's taking the curse are twofold. First, Gentiles receive *the blessing of Abraham* in the Messiah, which is justification by faith. And second, Jews receive *the promise of the Spirit through faith*. They could not get it by the law, but they could get it by *faith*, which is the content of the promise.

c. The Priority of Promise – 3:15-22

Paul continues the theological argument by showing the failure of legalism because of the priority of God's promises.

(1) The Law and the Abrahamic Covenant

To answer the question of the relationship of the Law of Moses to the Abrahamic Covenant, Paul begins with a human illustration in verse 15:

> *3:15Brethren, I speak after the manner of men: Though it be but a man's covenant, yet when it had been confirmed, no one makes it void, or adds thereto.*

Once a contract has been signed, no changes can be made. While additions could be added to it, none of these additions in any way could make the original null and void because the original has priority over the addition.

Paul then applies the illustration in verse 16:

> *3:16Now to Abraham were the promises spoken, and to his seed. He says not, And to seeds, as of many; but as of one, And to your seed, which is Messiah.*

The Abrahamic Covenant was the priority. The Abrahamic Covenant was a contract given to Abraham and to a specific seed—not to Ishmael, but to Isaac. The point of that choice was to teach that it would not come through the works of the law, but through the promise of faith, through *Yeshua* the Messiah. The point is that the Abrahamic Covenant has priority over the Mosaic Covenant.

(2) The Promise of the Abrahamic Covenant

3:17Now this I say: A covenant confirmed beforehand by God, the law, which came four hundred and thirty years after, does not disannul, so as to make the promise of none effect. 18For if the inheritance is of the law, it is no more of promise: but God had granted it to Abraham by promise.

Because the Abrahamic Covenant has priority over the Mosaic Covenant, it has never been annulled, but is still very much in effect. Verse 17 states that the Law of Moses was an addition because it came *four hundred and thirty years after* the Abrahamic Covenant was made, and the addition cannot in any way annul the promise of the original. The *promise* of the Abrahamic Covenant had priority over the law, and the promise was that justification would come by faith. Furthermore, the law was never intended to cancel out the sphere of faith, for the Spirit is given by faith, not by the law. In no way did the Mosaic Law annul *the promise* of the Abrahamic Covenant.

The result is in verse 18. The law cannot render the promise null and void: *For if the inheritance is of the law, it is no more of promise.* But God had already decreed that the inheritance of salvation would be by means of a promise, not by means of a law. The "gift" is the great gift of salvation, based upon faith.

(3) The Purpose of the Law of Moses

Having pointed out that the law was an addition that can in no way render the original null and void, the purpose of the law could not be to cancel out the fact that justification would come by faith. The question then is: "What was the purpose of the law?"

Paul makes four points in verse 19a:

3:19aWhat then is the law? It was added because of transgressions, till the seed should come to whom the promise has been made;

First, the law *was added*. The law was an addition to the Abrahamic Covenant and so had a definite beginning point; it was not always operative. Second, Paul states: *It was added because of transgressions.* The giving of the law had the specific purpose of showing sin for what sin is. This purpose of the law is also given in Romans 3:20 and 5:20. Third, Paul uses the word *till*. The very word *till*, or until, emphasizes the fact that the Mosaic Law was intended to be temporary. How temporary? This is brought out by his fourth point, *till the seed should come.* It was temporary; it was in effect only until the *seed* came. Once it came, the law would no longer be in effect. In verse 16, Paul identified the seed to be the Messiah. The law came to an end with the death of *Yeshua* the Messiah.

With the giving of the law there was a difference of administration, as Paul says in verses 19b-20:

> *3:19b and it was ordained through angels by the hand of a mediator.*
> *20 Now a mediator is not a mediator of one; but God is one.*

The law needed *a mediator*. A *mediator* is one who goes back and forth, and the law required two parties with two mediators for it to work. The two parties in this case were God and Israel, with the law between them.

Then Paul points out that there were stages by which the law was given. The law went from God to angels, from angels to Moses, and from Moses to Israel. An angel served as *mediator* on behalf of God, whereas Moses served as a *mediator* on behalf of the people. God was twice removed from the recipients of the law because angels and Moses were between God and Israel. The fact that angels were mediators in the giving of the law is also brought out by Acts 7:53 and Hebrews 2:2.

However, the seed came directly from God, and so this required only one mediator. Through the Messiah, God is still dealing directly with man. With the law, God was twice removed from the recipients; but with faith, God is directly involved. Again it shows the superiority of operating in the sphere of faith as over against operating in the sphere of the law.

Paul concludes with the results of the law in verses 21-22:

3:21Is the law then against the promises of God? God forbid: for if there had been a law given which could make alive, verily righteousness would have been of the law. 22But the scriptures shut up all things under sin, that the promise by faith in Yeshua Messiah might be given to them that believe.

In verse 21, he first shows what the law could not do. The law could not bring justification. The law was unable to produce faith. Law and faith are not contradictory, but simply have different purposes; they operate in different spheres. What the law could not do is produce faith.

What the law did do is *shut up all things under sin* in verse 22. The law made sin so clear that all were seen to be in sin and so *shut up* in the prison-house of sin. The law showed all men to be in sin. By using the term "under sin," he means they were "shut up on all sides by sin." That is what happens to those operating in the sphere of the law. Furthermore, the law made clear that salvation was by grace through faith in the Messiah. That is the sphere of faith: the promise of salvation is granted to sinners who believe.

d. The Superiority of Mature Faith – 3:23-4:7

What Paul is basically showing in these next verses is that a person trying to become righteous by works is spiritually immature and does not obtain spiritual adulthood through faith. He also points out that to go back to the law is to go back to a state of immaturity. The apostle makes five arguments in this section.

(1) The Intent of the Law

The law's intent was to bring us not to itself, but to the Lord, to the Messiah.

According to Galatians 3:23-24, there are two aspects of the law:

3:23But before faith came, we were kept in ward under the law, shut up unto the faith which should afterwards be revealed. 24So that the law is become our tutor to bring us unto Messiah, that we might be justified by faith.

In verse 23, Paul pictures the law as a jailer. What did the law do? It kept us *in ward*; it kept us in jail. The Greek word means that we were like a prisoner under a special military guard. The law is bondage and this bondage is the same as the "shutting up" of verse 22. Verse 25 states: *But now that faith is come ...* He is using the word *faith* in a dispensational sense, meaning that the Dispensation of law has ended and the Dispensation of Grace has now begun. Through the Messiah, we are free from the law. The law kept us imprisoned until faith came.

Not only is the law a jailer, the law is also a *tutor*, according to verse 24. The Greek word means "pedagogue." The ancient pedagogue was "a child-leader" and "a child-discipliner." The pedagogue was the custodian or the guardian of the child's education. He was to keep the child from evil by virtue of harsh disciplinary measures. The pedagogue's authority existed until the child became of age, and then his authority ended. Once an adult, the child was expected to do right voluntarily what he formerly did out of fear. If he did not follow what was right as an adult, the issue was no longer between the adult child and the pedagogue; it was now between the child and his father. Likewise, the law was a pedagogue *to bring us* to the Messiah. Again, the pronoun *us* refers to Jewish believers, for only the Jews were under the law. The law was to bring *us* Jews to the Messiah.

How would the law lead the Jews to the Messiah? It would lead them by commandments, ordinances, and laws. The commandments were God's standard of righteousness, and the law showed man's inability to obtain that righteousness. The only way out is to receive justification by some other means, and that is justification *by faith*. The ordinances were the ceremonial laws which showed that the person under the law was unclean, and to be cleansed required atonement by blood. The word "laws" applies to judicial laws. They would show that the penalty for breaking the law, the penalty for sin, was death.

In the end, under the law, one would conclude that there is no way we could possibly be justified by the law. There simply has to be another way.

In this way, the law would bring the Jewish believers to the Messiah. Through the Messiah, they would *be justified by faith*.

The three results of this justification are found in the next two verses:

> *3:25But now that faith is come, we are no longer under a tutor.* *26For ye are all sons of God, through faith, in Messiah Yeshua.*

First, faith has arrived; maturity has arrived. The law has accomplished its purpose in that we have arrived to faith.

Second, we no longer need *a tutor*, as the Law of Moses no longer has any authority over us. Its authority has ceased; we are now living in a brand-new era.

Third, we are now the *sons of God*; we are the children of God. We are born again, and therefore share God's nature because of our salvation. Being *sons of God* gives us a new legal status with certain rights and privileges; we attain to this sonship by means of faith, not by means of works. The content of our faith is *Yeshua* the Messiah. In the Messiah, we are sons, and our sonship-relationship with the Messiah is our position of being "in the Messiah." The law has led us to become the *sons of God*.

(2) The Entrance into the New Sphere

> *3:27For as many of you as were baptized into Messiah did put on Messiah.* *28There can be neither Jew nor Greek, there can be neither bond nor free, there can be no male and female; for ye all are one man in Messiah Yeshua.* *29And if ye are Messiah's, then are ye Abraham's seed, heirs according to promise.*

The means of entering this new sphere is by Spirit baptism, according to verse 27. This is in keeping with I Corinthians 12:13, that by *one Spirit were we all baptized into one body*. By Spirit baptism, we are placed *into* the Messiah; by being placed into the Messiah, we have *put on* the Messiah. We are now adults. In the ancient Greek and Roman custom, when a child was declared an adult, he put on the adult toga. Now that we are mature in the Messiah because we have exercised faith, we have *put on* the Messiah.

The subjects in verse 28 are both Jews and Gentiles. Paul is not saying here that all the distinctions between Jews and Gentiles have been erased. All he is saying in this context is that, as far as how one is justified, one is justified by grace through faith whether he is Jew or Gentile, bond or free, male or female. In other areas, of course, distinctions still remain, but in matters of salvation, all are on the same plane, needing only to be justified by faith.

In the Mosaic Law, there was a distinction. For example: Gentiles had to adopt Judaism; males, not females, had to offer sacrifices; free men, not slaves, had to offer sacrifices. In the sphere of law, there were distinctions in the realm of the works of the law. In the sphere of faith, there are no such distinctions: all are saved the same way. We all enter the Body in the same way, by means of Spirit baptism. Spiritual privileges come equally to all. However, unity does not mean uniformity. In position, we are the same, although in practice, there are differences. Distinctions between Jews and Gentiles remain, but not in the area of justification.

Then finally, he concludes with a result, in verse 29: those in faith are associated with Abraham. They are the sons of Abraham because they have been saved by faith. Believers are the Messiah's and are *Abraham's seed*, and they receive the *promise* of salvation by faith.

(3) The State of Immaturity

> *4:1But I say that so long as the heir is a child, he differs nothing from a bondservant though he is lord of all; 2but is under guardians and stewards until the day appointed of the father. 3So we also, when we were children, were held in bondage under the rudiments of the world:*

In verses 1-2, the apostle begins with a human illustration that as long as the child is a minor, he is of no more status than the servant. Even though he is *the heir* to all authority, as a minor, he has no more authority than a servant. In fact, he is even *under* the servant, *under* the pedagogue. He has no more freedom than a servant and in some situations even less. He is under others, like a servant is under others, and this status is continued until the father declares him to be a son and an heir. At that point, he is declared to be mature.

Paul then makes the application of that human illustration in verse three. "Under the law" means that as long as the Dispensation of law existed, we were minors who were *held in bondage*. The *bondage* was the legal observances of the law, the elementary teachings of a system of external observances and regulations. The bondage for the Gentiles had to do with pagan ritual. The word *rudiments* means the "ABC's," the simple things, the regulations of the law, which show immaturity. This was the point also made in Colossians 2:6-10 and Hebrews 5:11-14. During the law, we were held under bondage, in subjection, and in that sense, the law kept us in a state of spiritual immaturity.

(4) The Means to Maturity

Paul begins by showing the means to maturity:

> *4:4 but when the fulness of the time came, God sent forth his Son, born of a woman, born under the law, 5 that he might redeem them that were under the law, that we might receive the adoption of sons.*

In verse four, Paul talks about the coming of the Messiah. He declares, then, that in the *fulness of the time*—at a certain, set time, meaning at the anointed time for the fulfillment of the messianic prophecies—the Messiah came. The kind of redeemer that was necessary to rectify the situation under the law was the Jewish God-Man. There are the three key statements made about the Son. First, *God sent forth his Son*, emphasizing the Messiah's deity. Second, He was *born of a woman*, emphasizing the Messiah's humanity. Third, He was *born under the law*, emphasizing the Messiah's Jewishness. He was the Jewish God-Man, and God chose for Him to come—at a certain, fixed point in time.

In verse five, the purpose for His coming was twofold. He came for the Jewish people, to *redeem them that were under the law* for the Jews were under the law. The change of pronoun to *we* is noteworthy. That *we*—Jews and Gentiles together—*might receive the adoption of sons*. The means to maturity, then, was the coming of the Jewish God-Man, the Messiah.

(5) The Results of Maturity

4:6And because ye are sons, God sent forth the Spirit of his Son into our hearts, crying, Abba, Father. 7So that you are no longer a bondservant, but a son; and if a son, then an heir through God.

Paul deals with the three results of this maturity. In verse six, the first result is that we have the Spirit of God. *God sent forth the Spirit*, and the word *sent* emphasizes that He was sent for a specific mission. God *sent forth the Spirit . . . into our hearts.* This marks the locality, making us conscious of a new relationship. The same point is made in Romans 8:14-15 and 17. Our sonship with God means we can cry: *Abba, Father.* That is the magnitude of the Father-son relationship. The word *Abba* does not simply mean "father;" it is a more intimate term that means "daddy." It is the very way *Yeshua* addressed the Father in Mark 14:35-36. The Spirit is living within *our hearts*, addressing the Father the same way *Yeshua* did: *Abba, Father.* Furthermore, Romans 8:15 points out that believers also have the right to address the Father as *Abba*, as "Daddy." Because of our sonship-relationship with God the Father, we can approach Him on the basis of *Abba.* Romans 8:26 explains more about this relationship. The Holy Spirit cries: *Abba, Father*, and He cries *with groanings which cannot be uttered.* The Greek word used in Romans 8:26 means "to croak like a raven." Because He "croaks like a raven," His words cannot be verbally uttered.

In verse 7a, the second result of maturity is that we are no longer in bondage; we are adult sons. We are not the servants of the law, but servants of good works under the authority of God the Father. To go back under the law would be a sign of immaturity.

In verse 7b, the third result of maturity is that we are *an heir* of salvation. This is our position now: heirs of salvation.

e. The Danger of Reversion – 4:8-11

In the previous section, Paul taught that the Jews who were in bondage to the law had now been freed in the Messiah. In the next section, he teaches that the Gentiles were also in bondage but have also been freed in the Messiah.

(1) The Change of Status

4:8Howbeit at that time, not knowing God, ye were in bondage to them that by nature are no gods: 9but now that ye have come to know God, or rather to be known by God, how turn ye back again to the weak and beggarly rudiments, whereunto ye desire to be in bondage over again?

Paul begins by pointing out their changed status. In verse eight, he says their previous state was that they did not know God. They were *in bondage* to *no gods* and they were subjects to these *no gods* because of their many practices and rituals.

However, he continures in verse nine, they *have come to know God* in their new state. They have come to know Him by experience, which is the meaning of the Greek word for "knowing." Furthermore, they are *known by God* also *known* by experience. They are *known by God*, they *have come to know God*, and so the truth has set them free. Yet they are now turning back to bondage by going back to the formal ritualism from which they had been freed. These rituals are *weak*; they are impotent; they have no power to rescue them from condemnation. They are *beggarly* in that they bring neither spiritual riches nor spiritual blessing. To go back to ritualism is to go back to bondage.

(2) The Danger of Rituals

4:10Ye observe days, and months, and seasons, and years. 11I am afraid of you, lest by any means I have bestowed labor upon you in vain.

Paul enumerates some of the rituals they are going back to on the basis of the law in verse 10. They were observing *days*, the Sabbath; *months*, the new moon festival; *seasons*, the Jewish festivals; *years*, the Sabbatical Year and the Year of Jubilee. There is nothing wrong with observing these rituals on a voluntary basis, but they were making them mandatory, which would lead to bondage.

There is a real danger of reversion, according to verse 11. Paul labored to bring them out of bondage, but now he fears that, if they go back into bondage, he labored *in vain*.

f. A Contrast of Motives – 4:12-20

Paul continues the theological argument by showing the failure of legalism as a contrast of motives.

(1) The Motivation of Paul

The apostle begins with his own previous personal experiences with them and his own motivation and makes an appeal in verse 12:

> *4:12I beseech you, brethren, become as I am, for I also am become as ye are. Ye did me no wrong:*

"Be like me, be free!" Paul begs. The reason is that Paul once became like them, he identified with them, in order to bring them to the Messiah.

He reminds them of the circumstances that caused him to preach the gospel to them in verses 13-14:

> *4:13but ye know that because of an infirmity of the flesh I preached the gospel unto you the first time: 14and that which was a temptation to you in my flesh ye despised not, nor rejected; but ye received me as an angel of God, even as Messiah Yeshua.*

It was *an infirmity*, a physical illness, which forced him to stay in Galatia. While he was there, he preached the gospel to them. Paul's hideous look that this particular disease caused did not cause the Galatians to despise him. They received him *as an angel.* They received him with the same joy with which they would have received the Messiah Himself.

Now their attitude had changed, he writes in verse 15:

> *4:15Where then is that gratulation of yourselves? for I bear you witness, that, if possible, ye would have plucked out your eyes and given them to me.*

"Where is your joy now?" he asks. They have grown cold toward him. At one time, they would have sacrificed anything for him, but not now. They would have given him their eyes, but not now. This very statement may indicate what the physical problem was. It was a problem in relation to his eyesight; he hints at it again later, in Galatians 6:11.

He asks some rhetorical questions emphasizing why they had become cold to him in verse 16:

> *4:16So then am I become your enemy, by telling you the truth?*

He asks, "I have not become your enemy by telling you the truth, have I?" It is a rhetorical question which should require a "no" answer.

(2) The Motivation of the Judaizers

> *4:17They zealously seek you in no good way; nay, they desire to shut you out, that ye may seek them. 18But it is good to be zealously sought in a good matter at all times, and not only when I am present with you.*

Having spelled out his past experiences with them and the situation that caused him to preach the gospel, his own motive, Paul next describes the motive of the Judaizers. In verse 17, he accuses them of being zealous in a bad way, "For they are courting you in order to separate you from us and they only do it so that you will court their favor. You will now end up going to them rather than going to the Messiah."

In verse 18, Paul states that it is good to be *zealously sought* after, but it must be in a good way. The Judaizers are doing it for selfish motivation and selfish interests.

(3) Paul's Anguish

4:19My little children, of whom I am again in travail until Messiah be formed in you—20but I could wish to be present with you now, and to change my tone; for I am perplexed about you.

These verses clearly show his anguished attitude toward the Galatian believers. He calls them his *little children* in verse 19. This is the only time Paul uses this expression in all of his writings. It is more commonly used by the Apostle John. He refers to them as *my little children* because he led them to the Messiah; he is their spiritual father. There is a Jewish saying that if one teaches the son of his neighbor the Scriptures, it is reckoned as though he had begotten him. They are his children because he led them to the Lord, not the Judaizers. He uses birth imagery to ask, "Must I go through the whole process all over again to get you to see the necessity of living by faith alone?"

In verse 20, Pauls says he desires to be with them so that he can change his tone, because he is completely *perplexed* with the actions that the Galatian believers are now taking.

g. The Contrast of Bondage and Liberty: Galatians 4:21-31

The next point Paul makes in his theological argument shows the failure of legalism from the contrast of bondage and liberty:

21 Tell me, ye that desire to be under the law, do ye not hear the law?

Since the Galatians like rabbinic exegesis, Paul will give them some rabbinic exegesis. For those who desire to be under the law, they should consider if they really listen to the law.

²²For it is written, that Abraham had two sons, one by the handmaid, and one by the freewoman. ²³Howbeit the son by the handmaid is born after the flesh; but the son by the freewoman is born through promise.

Paul draws the contrast and begins by making a comparison between Abraham and the individual believer. Abraham received a promise of a son, the promise of a seed. The question now is how to obtain that promise. One option is to try to obtain it by works, which Abraham did by impregnating Hagar: Hagar was the means; Ishmael was the product; the result was that they were both cast out, because the promise was not to be obtained by human effort. Abraham then sought to obtain the promise by faith. This time Sarah was the means; Isaac was the product; the result was that the promise was fulfilled.

Applying Paul's comparison, the individual now has a promise of salvation. The question is how to obtain it. One option is by means of works, which in this context would be the works of the Mosaic Law; but the product is going to be legalism and condemnation; and the result will be bondage. The second option is to obtain the promise by faith; the means here is the Abrahamic Covenant as it is fulfilled by the New Covenant; the product will be justification; and the result will be salvation. Therefore, faith is the means.

h. Five Sets of Pairs – 4:24-27

²⁴Which things contain an allegory: for these women are two covenants; one from mount Sinai, bearing children unto bondage, which is Hagar. ²⁵Now this Hagar is mount Sinai in Arabia and answers to the Jerusalem that now is: for she is in bondage with her children. ²⁶But the Jerusalem that is above is free, which is our mother. ²⁷For it is written,
Rejoice, you barren that bears not;
Break forth and cry, you that travails not:
For more are the children of the desolate than of her that has the husband.

After making this comparison, he draws the allegory with five sets of pairs. The first set of pairs is the two women: Hagar and Sarah. The second set of pairs is the two sons: Ishmael and Isaac. The third set is the two covenants: Mosaic and Abrahamic. The fourth set is the two mountains: Sinai and Golgotha. And the fifth set is the two cities: Old Jerusalem and New Jerusalem.

In comparison, Hagar represents the Mosaic Covenant. Ishmael represents legalism. Mount Sinai represents the place where the people put themselves into bondage to the law. Old Jerusalem is the Jerusalem now in bondage. The destiny is to be cast out. But Sarah represents the Abrahamic Covenant. Isaac represents justification. Golgotha is where freedom was purchased. New Jerusalem is now free. Their destiny is to appear with the Son as a result. Those who accept the bondage of the law are rightfully children of Hagar, but those who exercise faith are the true sons of Abraham.

i. Paul's Conclusion – 4:28-31

Finally, Paul draws his conclusion, which is the result of liberty and of bondage:

> [28] *Now we, brethren, as Isaac was, are children of promise.* [29] *But as then he that was born after the flesh persecuted him that was born after the Spirit, so also it is now.* [30] *Howbeit what says the scripture? Cast out the handmaid and her son: for the son of the handmaid shall not inherit with the son of the freewoman.* [31] *Wherefore, brethren, we are not children of a handmaid, but of the freewoman.*

In verse 28, Pauls says the result of liberty is that we are now like Isaac; we are in the line of faith.

In verse 29, he then shows the relationship between the bond and the free. Ishmael persecuted Isaac when Isaac was weaned. Now, those who are under the law are persecuting those who are free. Non-believing Jewish people are persecuting Jewish believers.

According to verse 30, in the ultimate end of the conflict, legalism as a way of salvation is to be cast out, for the sphere of the law is bondage, but the sphere of faith is liberty.

> *The sphere of the law is bondage,*
> *but the sphere of faith is liberty.*

In verse 31, the application is that they are the children of *the freewoman,* and therefore, they should not go back into bondage. With this he concludes his second argument, the theological argument.

3. The Practical Argument – 5:1-6:10

Paul's third major argument for salvation by faith alone is the practical argument. In it, the apostle emphasizes the effects of liberty and makes five points.

a. The Introduction of the Argument – 5:1

For freedom did Messiah set us free: stand fast therefore, and be not entangled again in a yoke of bondage.

This is a summary statement that declares that *Yeshua* the Messiah has *set us free.* Therefore, Paul warns, "do not fall again into a state of spiritual bondage." The Greek word for "falling into bondage" means "to be ensnared in such a way so that you can never get out."

b. The Consequences of Liberty – 5:2-12

Having said that the Messiah has *set us free* and that we are not to fall into bondage again, Paul gives seven reasons for his summary statement that we should not be tied up into bondage again.

(1) Submission to Circumcision

> *5:2Behold, I Paul say unto you, that, if ye receive circumcision, Messiah will profit you nothing.*

In this verse, the apostle states that if they *receive circumcision* with a view to justification, it means that *Yeshua* has "profited them nothing," because circumcision—in view of justification by the works of the law—will lead automatically to a rejection of justification by faith. After being justified by faith, if they now go back to the law and are circumcised as an act of submission to the law, they will then deprive themselves of the ministry of the Spirit[1], for the Spirit was not provided through the law.

The act of circumcision will mean that they are trying to be saved by works and trying to be sanctified by works. Neither justification nor sanctification comes by means of works. While they will not lose their salvation, they will deprive themselves of the power available to them through the indwelling Spirit.

(2) Obligated to the Whole Law

> *5:3Yea, I testify again to every man that receives circumcision, that he is a debtor to do the whole law.*

If they are circumcised, they will be obligated *to do the whole law*. The believer is free from the law in three respects. First, the believer is free from the condemnation of the law to those who disobey (Gal. 3:10-13;

---

[1] This will be discussed in depth in chapter V on page 121.

Jas. 2:10). Second, the believer is free from the law as a means of justification (Gal. 3:11-12). And third, as this passage shows, the believer is free from any obligation to render obedience to the law. They are not obligated to keep any part of the law now that they have been justified by faith in the Messiah.

(3) Freedom in Messiah Rendered Inoperative

> *5:4 Ye are severed from Messiah, ye who would be justified by the law; ye are fallen away from grace.*

Going back to the law means that they have been *severed* from the Messiah. The question here is not grace and law, but grace or law. The Greek word translated as *severed* or "fallen away" is *katargeo*, which means "to render inoperative." He is not saying that they lose their salvation. What he is saying is that seeking either justification or sanctification by means of the law will render their relationship to the Messiah inoperative. This is the same Greek word that is used in Romans 7:2 and 6 in reference to the Mosaic Law; the law has been rendered inoperative.

Because going back to the law will render the relationship to the Messiah inoperative, they will not be able to rely on the Spirit to keep the righteousness of God. Instead, they are *fallen away from grace.* The word simply means "to fall short." It is used the same way in Hebrews 12:15. Again, it is not a statement that means they lose their salvation, but rather they will deprive themselves of the ministry of the Spirit.

The term "falling from grace" means that they will fall from the power given to them for daily living because one can work either in the sphere of the law or in the sphere of the Spirit; it is not both the law and the Spirit. They will, by being circumcised, go from the sphere of faith to the sphere of the law, and, in that sense, they will fall short of grace. But, again, Galatians 5:4 does not mean they will lose their salvation; it simply means that they will no longer be relying on the Spirit to live the spiritual life. One cannot operate in both spheres of faith and law; it is one or the other.

(4) Obtaining Righteousness by Faith

5:5For we through the Spirit by faith wait for the hope of righteousness.

Righteousness comes by the Spirit and not by the law. This is true for both justification and sanctification.

(5) Circumcision Avails Nothing in Messiah

5:6For in Messiah Yeshua neither circumcision avails anything, nor uncircumcision; but faith working through love.

No one is saved just because he is circumcised. No one is condemned just because he is not circumcised. What prevails is faith in the substitutionary death of the Messiah.

(6) The Source of this Doctrine

5:7Ye were running well; who hindered you that ye should not obey the truth? 8This persuasion came not of him that calls you.

Neither the doctrine of justification by law nor the doctrine of sanctification by law comes from God. Paul reminds them that they started out well, and he reminds them about what he said in Galatians 3:1-5: They had started out well, but now they have been *hindered* in their spiritual development. The reason they have been hindered is that they have gone away from the sphere of faith into the sphere of law.

(7) The Principle

5:9A little leaven leavens the whole lump.

If they pervert this aspect of salvation, they will eventually pervert the whole counsel of God.

(8) Paul's Position

5:10I have confidence to you-ward in the Lord, that ye will be none otherwise minded: but he that troubles you shall bear his judgment, whosoever he be.

After giving these seven reasons why they should not go back into bondage, Paul spells out his own position. He clearly states that he is confident that the Galatians will end up doing right, and furthermore, that the false teachers will receive their judgment, because teachers will receive a heavier judgment, according to James 3:1.

(9) Paul's Answer

5:11But I, brethren, if I still preach circumcision, why am I still persecuted? then has the stumbling-block of the cross been done away. 12I would that they that unsettle you would even go beyond circumcision.

As this section closes, Paul answers several accusations that were leveled against him. In verse 11a, the very fact that he was persecuted shows that he was not preaching circumcision. He was answering an accusation that he preaches circumcision to the Jews, but he does not preach circumcision to the Gentiles. The fact that he is being persecuted falsifies that claim.

If that were true, then the cross, as a stumbling-block, becomes inoperative according to verse 11b. According to I Corinthians 1:23, the cross is a stumbling-block to the Jewish people. It is a *stumbling-block* because it teaches freedom from the law; if circumcision is preached, it is no longer a *stumbling-block*. Of course, Paul does not preach circumcision.

In verse 12, Paul declares that those who do circumcise should go ahead and cut everything off because it will do no more good than cutting off only the foreskin. He is getting a little earthy here, but he is very strong in this position that no amount of circumcision, whether a small cutting or a great cutting, will do anything for justification or sanctification.

49

c. A Definition of Freedom – 5:13-15

[13]For ye, brethren, were called for freedom; only use not your freedom for an occasion to the flesh, but through love be servants one to another. [14]For the whole law is fulfilled in one word, even in this: You shall love your neighbor as yourself. [15]But if ye bite and devour one another, take heed that ye be not consumed one of another.

In these verses, Paul answers the question, "If one is saved by grace, does that mean he can do anything he wants to do?" That same question is raised in Romans 6:1-2. If they are truly saved by grace through faith plus nothing, and if nothing can render their salvation null and void, can they now do anything they want to do?

In verse 13, Paul points out that being free means that we cannot use our freedom for the purpose of sinning, but we use our freedom as it is guided by *love*, especially the love of the brethren. Freedom is to be guided by love; freedom means service, not license; freedom, exercised by love, means to become *servants one to another*.

In verse 14, Paul then gives a summary of the law. The true fulfillment of the law is to love one's neighbor as oneself. That was stated by *Yeshua* in Matthew 22:34-40. If one loves his neighbor as himself, this principle fulfills that which the law requires on a human level. The law did not provide, however, the capacity to love. But faith, through the power of the Spirit, does provide the capacity to love one's neighbor; therefore, that is what we should be doing.

Finally, in verse 15, he points out that failure to act on the basis of love results in mutual destruction: "You will *bite and devour one another* and you will be *consumed one of another*." In order to avoid self- destruction, what they need to be doing is loving one another. The next two sections are applications of how their freedom is to be practiced.

50

d. Individual Practice – 5:16-24

Paul deals with the individual practice in answering a question: "How do we live the victorious life?" He has already made it clear that one does not live it by going back to the law. Instead, he gives five other options.

(1) The Believer's Daily Walk

5:16But I say, Walk by the Spirit, and ye shall not fulfil the lust of the flesh.

The word *Spirit* in the Greek text does not have the definite article, which means that it could be taken in one of two ways. It might be the Holy Spirit or it might be the newborn or regenerated human spirit. The latter is to be preferred because the conflict between flesh and spirit is not between the flesh and the Holy Spirit. The conflict is between the flesh and the newborn human spirit. The conflict described here is the same conflict described in Romans 7:15-25, where it is clearly a conflict between the human flesh and the newborn or regenerated human spirit.

Furthermore, the Greek word for *walk* means "to accomplish one's daily tasks." The Greek tense emphasizes that one should be walking consistently on the basis of the newborn human spirit; one should live the spiritual life by reliance on the newborn spirit. One walks by reliance on the ability and the power of that newborn human spirit because it has been born again by virtue of being regenerated by the Holy Spirit. If we walk on the basis of our newborn human spirit, the result will be that we will *not fulfil the lust of the flesh.* Because the word *walk* has to do with daily tasks, it points to individual human practice.

(2) Concerning the Two Natures

5:17For the flesh lusts against the Spirit, and the Spirit against the flesh; for these are contrary the one to the other; that ye may not do the things that ye would.

This verse describes the two capacities within the believer and teaches one to be aware of the conflict within him. He still has the "old man," *the flesh*, but he also has the newborn human spirit; and the two natures, the old nature and the new nature, are in conflict with one another.

The unsaved person has only one nature, only one capacity, and that is to serve and please himself. But the believer has two capacities. The believer has an option. He can walk either on the basis of *the flesh*, the old nature, or on the basis of the spirit, the new nature. The same person has a new capacity to serve God with righteousness.

The thing to remember is that the two capacities are at war, and because they are at war, the believer always acts either on the basis of one capacity or the other. Every act he does is either on the basis of the old nature or the new nature. It is this inner conflict that will keep one from ever obtaining perfection under the law (Rom. 7:15-25), because the law is the sin nature's base of operation. So one is to be aware of the conflict that is within himself.

(3) How to Live the Victorious Life

5:18But if ye are led by the Spirit, ye are not under the law.

Believers are to remember their liberty: they are *led by the Spirit*. As a believer, if one is led by the spirit, he is not under the law.

(4) The Results of the Two Natures

5:19Now the works of the flesh are manifest, which are these: fornication, uncleanness, lasciviousness, 20idolatry, sorcery, enmities, strife, jealousies, wraths, factions, divisions, parties, 21envyings, drunkenness, revellings, and such like; of which I forewarn you, even as I did forewarn you, that they who practise such things shall not inherit the kingdom of God. 22But the fruit of the Spirit is love, joy, peace, longsuffering, kindness, goodness, faithfulness, 23meekness, self-control; against such there is no law.

Paul begins by listing the results of *the works of the flesh* in verses 19-21. All of these are actions *of the flesh,* and those who operate in the flesh will serve or reflect these very things. He categorizes them in four areas:

1. **Sensual Actions:** *fornication* (prostitution), *uncleanness* (moral impurity), and *lasciviousness* (promiscuity; such as, pre-marital or extra-marital sexual relationships and things of that nature)
2. **False worship:** *idolatry* and *sorcery* (witchcraft)
3. **Personal and social relations:** *enmities* (personal animosities), *strife* (rivalry and discord), *jealousies* (of an unnatural kind), *wraths* (people being vengeful toward one another), *factions,* (divisions within the Body), *divisions* (among individuals and within married couples), *parties* (heresies), *envyings* (feelings of ill will)
4. **Intemperance:** *drunkenness* and *revellings* (orgies)

Having listed all these things, he points out that people *who practise such things* will not *inherit* the Kingdom of God. While these works are common among the unsaved, saved people, of course, can also fall into these sins.

While all will enter the Messianic Kingdom, not all will *inherit* the Messianic Kingdom, meaning not all will be rewarded and receive a position of honor and glory in the Kingdom. So how we live now does matter and will matter for a thousand years. These works in believers do not mean that they will not enter the Kingdom, but it does mean that they are not walking on the basis of the newborn human spirit. Believers may indeed fall into these sins, but, if they are true believers, they will be dealt with by God in such a way that they will either repent or they will be taken by divine discipline to Heaven early.

After listing these various results of walking in the old nature, Paul then mentions the results of walking on the basis of the new nature, the newborn human spirit. In verses 22-23, he mentions nine things which are usually referred to as *the fruit of the Spirit.* But again, these are not the fruit of the Holy Spirit, they are the fruit of the newborn human spirit. Of course, the newborn human spirit is newborn because it was regenerated by the Holy Spirit, so the Holy Spirit is ultimately responsible. However, as far as a direct cause-and-effect relationship here, we are dealing with the newborn human spirit.

These nine results are: *love, joy, peace, long suffering* (patience), *kindness* (emphasizing an attitude or spirit of kindness), *goodness* (good deeds), *faithfulness, meekness, self-control.* These nine results of the newborn human spirit counteract the results of the old flesh mentioned in verses 19-21.

(5) How to Live the Spiritual Life

5:24 And they that are of Messiah Yeshua have crucified the flesh with the passions and the lusts thereof.

The fifth answer as to how they live the spiritual life is to regard the flesh as once-and-for-all dead. Positionally speaking—on the basis of positional truth—they are to view the flesh as being dead. Positionally, the flesh is dead, but experientially there is a struggle between the two capacities, as Paul has pointed out in verse 17, and as he also points out in Romans 6:6. He details the struggle in Romans 7:15-25. Positionally, the flesh is dead, but experientially, there is a struggle between the two capacities.

Those who are in *Yeshua* the Messiah *have crucified the flesh.* Therefore, the believer, unlike the unbeliever, does have the power and the capacity to operate and to walk on the basis of the newborn human spirit. The unbeliever has no choice. Having such a choice, the admonition is: "Let us walk on the basis of the newborn human spirit, and let us produce the ninefold fruit of this newborn human spirit in our daily living."

e. Social Practice – 5:25-6:10

In this section, Paul points out the social practice as he applies the principle of daily living to society rather than to individual practice, as he did earlier.

(1) The Exhortation to Keep in Step

5:25 If we live by the Spirit, by the Spirit let us also walk.

Paul begins with the exhortation, "Since, positionally, we are already living in the spirit, let us also walk in the spirit." For the second time Paul tells them to *walk* by the spirit. The first time was in verse 16; he now tells them again in verse 25.

In the Greek, there are two different words used. In verse 16, Paul used a Greek word that has to do with the physical act of walking; it has to do with daily walking, daily tasks, and daily activities. Therefore, in verses 15-24, he was dealing with individual practice.

The Greek word used in verse 25 is a military term for "keeping in step," "keeping in step with other soldiers." If one does not keep in step when marching, he will begin tripping up the others. Here Paul deals with keeping in step with others; therefore, what he has to say in the following verses has to do with social practice rather than with personal, individual practice.

(2) Ways of Keeping in Step

After having given us the exhortation to keep in step with the spirit in all the details of their lives—to keep in step with the spirit and with others—he then goes on to give seven ways of keeping in step.

(a) Do Not Seek Worldly Honor

5:26Let us not become vainglorious, provoking one another, envying one another.

They are exhorted not to seek worldly honor or to indulge in vain bragging because that will result in being out of sync with others and causing provocations.

(b) Do the Ministry of Restoration

6:1Brethren, even if a man be overtaken in any trespass, ye who are spiritual, restore such a one in a spirit of gentleness; looking to yourself, lest you also be tempted.

This is a case of another believer who has fallen out of step because he has been overpowered by sin. This is not dealing with a deliberate sin, but falling because of weakness. Paul says that those *who are spiritual* are to do the ministry of restoration. It is not just any believer who should perform this ministry, but those *who are spiritual*.

According to Scripture, there are four different types of people. First is *the natural man*, which is the unsaved man (I Cor. 2:14). The second type is the *babe in the Messiah* (I Cor. 3:1-3; Eph. 4:14; Heb. 5:13). These are new believers who still need the milk of the Word of God and are not ready for the meat of the Word of God. The third type of person is the *carnal man* who has been saved long enough to have matured but has failed to do so (I Cor. 3:1-3). The fourth type of person is the *spiritual* man, one who is a mature believer and who is walking regularly on the basis of his newborn human spirit in individual practice and also is walking and marching in step in social practice (I Cor. 2:15; 14:37-38; Heb. 5:14). It is this fourth type of individual—the spiritual one—who is responsible for restoring a believer who has fallen out of step. He is to use *a spirit of gentleness*, not a spirit of condemnation. At the same time, he should always remain on spiritual guard of himself, lest he, too, should find himself falling out of step.

(c) Bear One Another's Burdens

6:2 *Bear ye one another's burdens, and so fulfil the law of Messiah.*

The Greek word for *burdens* means "heavy weight." It is a weight that is simply too heavy for one person to carry, as it will overwhelm the man if he is not helped. This means that they are to help one another when a believer is overpowered either by sin or by circumstances. The result is that, in this way, they shall be fulfilling the *law of Messiah*, because the believer—as has been pointed out many times in this book—is no longer under the Law of Moses. He is under the law of the Messiah. The way they fulfill the law of the Messiah is by fulfilling the commandments of the New Testament, such as bearing one another's *burdens*.

(d) Bear Our Own Burden

^{6:3}*For if a man thinks himself to be something when he is nothing, he deceives himself. ⁴But let each man prove his own work, and then shall he have his glorying in regard of himself alone, and not of his neighbor. ⁵For each man shall bear his own burden.*

In verse three, Paul states that they are not to form an improper estimate of themselves, but in verse four, they are to lead such a life that it may be examined and it may be known exactly where they stand. In verse five, the reason for this is that everyone will be responsible for carrying *his own burden.* This is not a contradiction of verse two, which states that they must "carry one another's burdens," because two different Greek words are used. The word for *burden* in verse two is *baros* and has to do with a very heavy weight that no individual can carry without help. The Greek word used in verse five is *phortion* and means "a normal workload that any man could carry." It has to do with the normal load of one's responsibility. Everyone is required to fulfill his own individual responsibility. Everyone, in this sense, must carry his own weight.

(e) Share Material Goods

^{6:6}*But let him that is taught in the word communicate unto him that teaches in all good things.*

The Bible student should share his material goods with the Bible teacher, and this is another way of bearing one another's burdens. The point is that if one is benefiting spiritually from any teacher—be he a pastor, a Sunday School teacher, an author, or a radio teacher—if one is being blessed by these ministries, if he is learning Scripture from them, then he is obligated to share his material goods with the teacher. He should be financially supporting those from whom he is receiving spiritual benefits.

(f) Sow Properly

^{6:7}*Be not deceived; God is not mocked: for whatsoever a man sows, that shall he also reap. ⁸For he that sows unto his own flesh shall of*

the flesh reap corruption; but he that sows unto the Spirit shall of the Spirit reap eternal life.

If one sows to the *flesh,* he will reap the results of the flesh, listed in Galatians 5:19-21. But if one sows to the spirit, he will reap the results of Galatians 5:22-23, the fruit of the newborn human spirit.

(g) Do Good to All Men

⁶:⁹And let us not be weary in well-doing: for in due season we shall reap, if we faint not. ¹⁰So then, as we have opportunity, let us work that which is good toward all men, and especially toward them that are of the household of the faith.

There should be a special emphasis on doing good to those who are also believers. One can give charity to all men, but if he has to make a choice, the choice should be to a believing charity rather than to a secular one.

D. THE CONCLUSION: GALATIANS 6:11-18

As Paul draws his conclusions, he begins by spelling out the motive of liberty and states that he is now writing with his *own hand* in verse 11:

See with how large letters I write unto you with my own hand.

Paul often used a scribe to write a letter (Rom. 16:22), but wrote the closing himself (I Cor. 16:21; Col. 4:18; II Thes. 3:17). It would not be unusual that, after dictating this letter to a scribe, he now begins to write the closing himself *with* [his] *own hand.*

However, the way the verse is worded, it is not really clear that this is what he is saying. There are two possible options in the way this verse could be understood. The first option is that only now he begins to write the letter himself, having dictated the earlier portions of it. Or, second, he has written the whole letter with his own hand, but now draws attention to

58

the large letters, which may again imply the problem with eyesight. In any case, he is emphasizing the fact that he wants to draw their attention to the conclusions that he is now going to make.

1. False and Proper Motives – 6:12-15

Starting with the false motives of the Judaizers, he states three things that motivate the Judaizers in verses 12-13:

> *12As many as desire to make a fair show in the flesh, they compel you to be circumcised; only that they may not be persecuted for the cross of Messiah. 13For not even they who receive circumcision do themselves keep the law; but they desire to have you circumcised, that they may glory in your flesh.*

First, they want to *glory in your flesh*; they want to be able to report how many Gentiles have been circumcised. Second, they want to avoid the persecution of the cross. To preach that the cross is sufficient and that one does not need anything else but the cross results in persecution. To preach both law and the cross brought almost no persecution because then they could remain merely a sect within Judaism. Third, they do not keep the law themselves. Even those today who insist that evangelical believers must keep the law do not keep the law. They always have to make all kinds of adjustments because no one keeps the law in its entirety or in the way it is written. There are great portions of the law which everyone ignores no matter how ardent they are about keeping it. So the Judaizers are characterized by totally false motives.

The proper motive, by which Paul operated, was glorying in the cross alone, according to verse 14:

> *But far be it from me to glory, save in the cross of our Lord Yeshua Messiah, through which the world has been crucified unto me, and I unto the world.*

Paul is saying that through the cross, the world is crucified to them and they are crucified to the world.

He then draws his conclusion concerning circumcision and what the right criterion is in verse 15:

For neither is circumcision anything, nor uncircumcision, but a new creature.

As a basis of salvation, *circumcision* means nothing and *uncircumcision* means nothing. What counts is being a new creation, being a *new creature*, which means being regenerated through the cross. Regeneration through the cross frees one from the law because we are dead to the law and no longer have any obligation to keep it. Circumcision is necessary for Jewish believers in keeping with the Abrahamic Covenant; it is a necessary obedience, just as baptism is necessary for obedience. But neither circumcision nor baptism is a requirement for salvation. Neither circumcision nor baptism will avail in the area of justification or sanctification.

2. The Israel of God – 6:16

For those who follow the rule that circumcision is nothing and uncircumcision is nothing, but what matters is the cross of *Yeshua*, there is, Paul says in Galatians 6:16, peace and *mercy* for two separate groups:

And as many as walk by this rule, peace be upon them, and mercy, and upon the Israel of God.

First, he declares peace and mercy upon *them*. Who are the *them*? They are the Gentile believers to whom he has been writing. Second, he declares peace and mercy upon *the Israel of God*. Who is *the Israel of God*? It is not the Church. The *Israel of God* refers to Jewish believers, the believing Remnant within and among the Jewish people. One must never make the mistake of identifying *the Israel of God* with the Church or with Gentile believers as being some kind of new "spiritual Jews." This is not taught anyplace in Scripture. There are two different groups in this verse separated by the word *and*: first, *them*, who are the Gentile believers; second, *and . . . the Israel of God*, who are the Jewish believers.

Galatians 6:16 is vitally important to Covenant Theology and other forms of Replacement Theology since it is the only passage that even remotely could be interpreted to indicate that the Church is Israel. Therefore, it requires a more detailed treatment: [2]

The Book of Galatians is concerned with Gentiles who were attempting to attain salvation through the law. The ones deceiving them were Judaizers, who were Jews demanding adherence to the Law of Moses. To them, a Gentile had to convert to Judaism before he qualified for salvation through Christ. In verse 15, Paul states that the important thing for salvation is faith, resulting in the new man. He also mentions two elements: circumcision and uncircumcision. This refers to two groups of people: Jews and Gentiles, two groups already mentioned by these very terms in 2:7-9:

> *[7]but contrariwise, when they saw that I had been intrusted with the gospel of the uncircumcision, even as Peter with the gospel of the circumcision [8](for he that wrought for Peter unto the apostleship of the circumcision wrought for me also unto the Gentiles); [9]and when they perceived the grace that was given unto me, James and Cephas and John, they who were reputed to be pillars, gave to me and Barnabas the right hands of fellowship, that we should go unto the Gentiles, and they unto the circumcision;*

In verse 16, Paul then pronounces a blessing on members of the two groups who would follow this rule of salvation through faith alone. The first group is the *them*, the *uncircumcision*, the Gentile Christians to and of whom he

---

[2] The following text was first published in Fruchtenbaum, Arnold G. *Israelology: The Missing Link in Systematic Theology.* Tustin, CA: Ariel Ministries, 1993, pages 690-699, and is presented here with minor edits.

had devoted most of the epistle. The second group is the *Israel of God*. These are the *circumcision*, the Jewish believers who, in contrast with the Judaizers, followed the rule of salvation by grace through faith alone. Covenant Theologians must ignore the primary meaning of *kai*, which separates the two groups in the verse, in order to make them both the same group.

Dr. S. Lewis Johnson, former professor of Greek and New Testament Exegesis at Dallas Theological Seminary, has done a detailed study of Galatians 6:16. In his introduction, Johnson makes the following observation:

> In spite of overwhelming evidence to the contrary, persistent support remains for the contention that the term *Israel* may refer properly to Gentile believers in the present age... the primary support is found in Galatians 6:16 ...
>
> I cannot help but think that dogmatic considerations loom large in the interpretation of Galatians 6:16. The tenacity with which this application of "the Israel of God" to the church is held in spite of a mass of evidence to the contrary leads one to think that the supporters of the view believe their eschatological system, usually an amillennial scheme, hangs on the reference of the term to the people of God, composed of both believing Jews and Gentiles. Amillennialism does not hang on this interpretation, but the view does appear to have a treasured place in amillennial exegesis.
>
> In speaking of the view that the term refers to ethnic *Israel*, a sense that the term Israel has in every other of its more than sixty-five uses in the NT and in its fifteen uses in Paul, in tones almost emotional William Hendriksen, the respected Reformed commentator, writes, "I refuse to accept that explanation."...
>
> What I am leading up to is expressed neatly by D. W. B. Robinson in an article written about twenty years ago: "The glib citing of Gal. v.16 to support the view that 'the church

is the new Israel' should be vigorously challenged. There is weighty support for a limited interpretation." We can say more than this, in my opinion. There is more than weighty support for a more limited interpretation. There is overwhelming support for such. In fact, the least likely view among several alternatives is the view that "the Israel of God" is the church.[3]

Johnson presents three views concerning this verse. Only the first insists that the *Israel of God* is the Church as a whole while the other two limit it to Jewish believers. The first view is described as follows:

> The first is the claim that "the Israel of God" is simply a term descriptive of the believing church of the present age... The Israel of God is the body who shall walk by the rule of the new creation, and they include believing people from the two ethnic bodies of Jews and Gentiles.[4]

The basis for the first view is:

> The list of names supporting this view is impressive, although the bases of the interpretation are few and feeble, namely, the claim that the *kai* ... before the term "the Israel of God" is an explicative or appositional *kai*;... and the claim that if one sees the term "the Israel of God" as a believing ethnic Israel, they would be included in the

---

[3] Johnson Jr, S. Lewis. Paul and 'The Israel of God': An Exegetical and Eschatological Case-Study. The Master's Seminary Journal 20(1):41-55 Spring 2009, pp 41-43. Quoting in this section Hendriksen, William. *Exposition of Galatians.* Grand Rapids, Michigan: Baker Book House, 1968, p. 247, and Robinson, Donald WB. "The distinction between Jewish and Gentile believers in Galatians." *Australian Biblical Review* 13 (1965): 29-48.

[4] Ibid., p. 43.

preceding clause, "And those who will walk by this rule, peace and mercy be upon them."[5]

Johnson rejects this view on three grounds. The first is for grammatical and syntactical reasons for which there are two.[6] The first is that this view must resort to a secondary or lesser meaning of *kai*:

> It is necessary to begin this part of the discussion with a reminder of a basic, but often neglected, hermeneutical principle. It is this: in the absence of compelling exegetical and theological considerations, we should avoid the rarer grammatical usages when the common ones make good sense.[7]

> Because the latter usage serves well the view that the term "the Israel of God" is the church, the dogmatic concern overcame grammatical usage. An extremely rare usage has been made to replace the common usage, even in spite of the fact that the common and frequent usage of *and* makes perfectly good sense in Galatians 6:16.[8]

Second, Johnson points out that if Paul's intention was to identify the *them* as being the *Israel of God*, then the best way of showing this was to eliminate the *kai* altogether. [...] The very presence of the *kai* argues against the *them* being the *Israel of God*. As Johnson notes, "Paul, however, did not eliminate the *kai*."[9]

---

[5] Ibid., pp. 44-45.

[6] Ibid., pp. 47-49.

[7] Ibid., pp. 47-48.

[8] Ibid., p. 48.

[9] Ibid., p. 49.

The second ground for rejecting this view is for exegetical considerations, which deals with context and usage. Concerning usage, Johnson states:

> From the standpoint of biblical usage this view stands condemned. There is no instance in biblical literature of the term *Israel* being used in the sense of the church, or the people of God as composed of both believing ethnic Jews and Gentiles. Nor, on the other hand, as one might expect if there were such usage, does the phrase *ta ethné* (KJV, "the Gentiles") ever mean the non-Christian world specifically, but only the non-Jewish peoples, although such are generally non-Christians. Thus, the usage of the term *Israel* stands overwhelmingly opposed to the first view.
>
> The usage of the terms *Israel* and *the church* in the early chapters of the book of Acts is in complete harmony, for Israel exists there alongside the newly formed church, and the two entities are kept separate in terminology.[10]

For those who would cite Romans 9:6 as evidence, Johnson shows that this verse is no support for such a view, for the distinction is between Jews who believe and Jews who do not:

> Paul is here speaking only of a division within ethnic Israel. Some of them are believers and thus truly Israel, whereas others, though ethnically Israelites, are not truly Israel, since they are not elect and believing ... No Gentiles are found in the statement at all.[11]

---

[10] Ibid., p. 49.

[11] Ibid., pp. 49-50.

Even many Covenant Theologians have agreed with this view of Romans 9:6 and do not use it to support their view of Galatians 6:16. As for context, Johnson observes:

> On the contrary, the apostle is concerned with correcting the gospel preached to the Galatians by the Judaizers, particularly their false contention that it was necessary to be circumcised to be saved and to observe as Christians certain requirements of the Law of Moses in order to remain in divine favor ... The apostle makes no attempt whatsoever to deny that there is a legitimate distinction of race between Gentile and Jewish believers in the church.... There is a remnant of Jewish believers in the church according to the election of grace.... This approach fails to see that Paul does not say there is neither Jew nor Greek within the church. He speaks of those who are "in Christ."... But Paul also says there is neither male nor female, nor slave nor free man in Christ. Would he then deny sexual differences within the church? Or the social differences in Paul's day? Is it not plain that Paul is not speaking of national or ethnic difference in Christ, but of spiritual status? In that sense there is no difference in Christ.[12]

The third ground for rejecting this view is theological:

> ... no historical evidence points to that the term *Israel* being identified with the church before A.D. 160. Further, at that date there was no characterization of the church as "the Israel of God." In other words, for more than a century after Paul there was no evidence of the identification.[13]

---

[12] Ibid., p. 50.

[13] Ibid., p. 51.

Johnson's summary concerning the rejection of the first view is:

> To conclude the discussion of the first interpretation, it seems clear that there is little evidence—grammatical, exegetical, or theological—that supports it. On the other hand, there is sound historical evidence against the identification of *Israel* with believing or unbelieving Gentiles. The grammatical usage of *kai* is not favorable to the view, nor is the Pauline or NT usage of *Israel*. Finally, ... the Pauline teaching in Galatians contains a recognition of national distinctions in the one people of God.[14]

The second view is that the *Israel of God* is the believing Jewish remnant within the Church. This is Johnson's own view and is the common dispensational view. Johnson describes this view as follows:

> The second of the important interpretations of Galatians 6:16 and "the Israel of God" is the view that the words refer simply to believing ethnic Israelites in the Christian church. Does not Paul speak of himself as an Israelite (cf. Rom. 11:1)? And does not the apostle also speak of "a remnant according to God's gracious choice" (cf. 11:5), words that plainly in the context refer to believing Israelites? What more fitting thing could Paul write, it is said, in a work so strongly attacking Jewish professing believers, the Judaizers, than to make it most plain that he was not attacking the true believing Jews? Judaizers are anathematized, but the remnant according to the election of grace are "the Israel of God."...
>
> Perhaps this expression, "the Israel of God," contrasts with his expression in 1 Corinthians 10:18, "Israel after the flesh" (KJV), as the true, believing Israel versus the unbelieving

---

[14] Ibid., p. 51.

element, just as in Romans 9:6, the apostle distinguishes two Israels, one elect and believing, the other unbelieving, but both ethnic Israelites (cf. [Romans 9] vv. 7–13).[15]

Johnson supports this view on the same three grounds that he rejected the first view. On grammatical and syntactical grounds, Johnson states that "there are no grammatical, or syntactical considerations that would be contrary" to this view and, furthermore, the "common sense of *kai* as continuative, or copulative is followed."[16] In other words, it uses the primary meaning of *kai*.

On exegetical grounds Johnson states:

> Exegetically the view is sound, since "Israel" has its uniform Pauline ethnic sense. And further, the apostle achieves a very striking climactic conclusion. Drawing near the end of his "battle-epistle" with its harsh and forceful attack on the Judaists and its omission of the customary words of thanksgiving, Paul tempers his language with a special blessing for those faithful believing Israelites who, understanding the grace of God and its exclusion of any human works as the ground of redemption, had not succumbed to the subtle blandishments of the deceptive Judaizers. They, not the false men from Jerusalem, are "the Israel of God," or, as he calls them elsewhere, "the remnant according to the election of grace" (cf. Rom. 11:5).[17]

As for theological grounds, Johnson states:

---

[15] Ibid., p. 45.

[16] Ibid., p. 51.

[17] Ibid., p. 52.

And theologically the view is sound in its maintenance of the two elements within the one people of God, Gentiles and ethnic Jews. Romans 11 spells out the details of the relationship between the two entities from Abraham's day to the present age and on to the fulfillment in the future of the great unconditional covenantal promises made to the patriarchs.[18]

The third view agrees with the second, that the *Israel of God* must refer to Jewish believers and not the Church as a whole but sees this Jewish remnant as still future:

> The third of the interpretations is the view that the expression "the Israel of God" is used eschatologically and refers to the Israel that shall turn to the Lord in the future in the events that surround the second advent of our Lord. Paul would then be thinking along the lines of his well-known prophecy of the salvation of "all Israel" in Romans 11:25–27.[19]

> The third view ... takes the term "the Israel of God" to refer to ethnic Israel but locates their blessing in the future...[20]

Johnson has no major objections to the third view for "Grammatically and syntactically, this last option is sound."[21] Theologically, this view is also sound for:

---

[18] Ibid., p. 52.

[19] Ibid., p. 46.

[20] Ibid., p. 52.

[21] Ibid., p. 53.

... the view harmonizes with the important Pauline teaching that there are two kinds of Israelites, a believing one and an unbelieving one.[22]

The only real problem is exegetical, since "...the eschatological perspective ... has not been one of the major emphases of the Galatian epistle as a whole..."[23] However, Johnson allows for the exegetical possibility of this view for the wider context did mention the Abrahamic Covenant and the Kingdom of God.

The second view is probably the best. While the third is biblically acceptable, the first view is not. Johnson concludes:

> If there is an interpretation that totters on a tenuous foundation, it is the view that Paul equates the term "the Israel of God" with the believing church of Jews and Gentiles. To support it, the general usage of the term *Israel* in Paul, in the NT, and in the Scriptures as a whole is ignored. The grammatical and syntactical usage of the conjunction *kai* is strained and distorted—and the rare and uncommon sense accepted when the usual sense is unsatisfactory—only because it does not harmonize with the presuppositions of the exegete. And to compound matters, in the special context of Galatians and the general context of the Pauline teaching, especially as highlighted in Romans 11, Paul's primary passages on God's dealings with Israel and the Gentiles, are downplayed... the doctrine that the church of Gentiles and Jews is *the* Israel of God rests on an illusion. It is a classic case of tendentious exegesis.[24]

---

[22] Ibid., pp. 53-54.

[23] Ibid., p. 53.

[24] Ibid., p. 54.

The conclusion is that the Church is never called, and is not, a "spiritual Israel" or a "new Israel." The term *Israel* is either used of the nation or the people as a whole, or of the believing Remnant within. It is never used of the Church in general or of Gentile believers in particular.

3. Paul's Final Remarks – 6:17-18

In Galatians 6:17, Paul summarizes the persecution he has received for preaching the cross apart from the law:

Henceforth, let no man trouble me; for I bear branded on my body the marks of Yeshua.

The kinds of persecutions that had marked his body are spelled out in detail in II Corinthians 11:22-28. There were also special *marks* that were given to four categories of people in those days.

Soldiers were marked with a mark of allegiance; they were marked with the name of their commander. Paul was a soldier of the cross, and he was marked with the name of his commander, *Yeshua* of Nazareth.

Slaves were marked with a mark of ownership; they had the name of the owner. Paul many times called himself a "bond-slave of the Messiah" and he was owned by his master, *Yeshua*.

Criminals were marked with a mark of exposure; they had marked upon their body the name of the crime. Paul was treated and marked as a criminal for preaching *Yeshua*.

Devotees to various gods were marked with a mark of consecration; they were marked by the name of their particular god. Paul was a devotee to the Messiah and was marked with that name.

So Paul had all four marks on his body, and these marks were the result of the persecutions he had suffered.

Finally, he closes the letter with a benediction of liberty in Galatians 6:18:

The grace of our Lord Yeshua Messiah be with your spirit, brethren. Amen.

The grace is the means by which we are saved, by *grace* through faith. It is also the basis upon which we are to walk. It is this *grace* that has regenerated our human spirit. Therefore, we should walk by the spirit. With these words, the Book of Galatians closes.

Chapter IV – The Law of Moses and the Law of Messiah

The questions that plagued the believers nearly 2,000 years ago are still relevant today. Though we have Paul's epistle to the Galatians, there are still many believers who are uncertain about the role of the Law of Moses. How this law relates to believers is a very, very crucial issue. This is a problem especially for Jewish believers. The purpose of this chapter is to deal with the Scriptures from a Jewish as well as a messianic believer's perspective.

If there is one immediate problem that seems to face the new Jewish believer in the Messiah, it is his relationship to the Law of Moses. This tends to be more of a problem to the Jewish believers outside of Israel than to those in Israel, but every Jewish believer faces it to some measure. Generally speaking, it could be said that the average American messianic believer concurs with a partial keeping of the law, while the average Israeli believer concurs with the keeping of all of it, excluding those parts dealing with the Temple and its functions. This is at best an oversimplification. But regardless of the extent, the dilemma is the same: To what extent is the messianic believer to keep the Law of Moses?

Two factors have developed in the minds and teachings of many believers that have contributed to the creation of this problem. One is the practice of dividing the law into ceremonial, legal, and moral commandments. On the basis of this division, many have come to think that the believer is free from the ceremonial and legal commandments, but is still under the moral commandments. The second factor is the belief that the Ten Commandments are still valid today, while the other 603 commandments are not. When confronted by a Seventh-Day Adventist, the individual taking this approach runs into problems concerning the fourth commandment on keeping the Sabbath. At that point, "fudging" begins and results in inconsistency.

The Law of Moses poses a major problem for the messianic believer. The solution lies in discovering what the Bible says about his relationship to the law, especially the Ten Commandments.

One thing to point out is the means by which the Mosaic Law was given. Everyone knows that Moses received the law on Mount Sinai from the hand of God. Ten of those commandments, those written on the tablets of stone, were written with *the finger* of God. The other 603 were written down as Moses was commanded by God.

However, there is a Jewish legend and a Jewish tradition that says Moses received the law by means of angels. If one reads through the Old Testament, he will never see that anywhere, for there is not one place in the Old Testament where it is written that Moses received the law by means of angels. Yet this has been a very persistent Jewish and rabbinic teaching. Of course, there are many things in Jewish traditions, legends, or teachings that are not validated by the Scriptures. Sometimes they go contrary to the Scriptures. Then again, there are some things contained in Jewish legends and traditions that are validated by the New Testament. One of these is the particular tradition that Moses received the law from God by means of angels. The New Testament validates this in three different places: Acts 7:53, Galatians 3:19, and Hebrews 2:2.

In Acts 7:53, Paul explains that the Jewish people received the law, but it was ordained by means of angels:

ye who received the law as it was ordained by angels, and kept it not.

In Galatians 3:19, he repeats this claim:

What then is the law? It was added because of transgressions, till the seed should come to whom the promise has been made; and it was ordained through angels by the hand of a mediator.

For the second time, the New Testament validates the Jewish tradition that the Law of Moses was mediated, given to Moses, by means of angels. In the Book of Hebrews, a letter written specifically to Jewish believers, the tradition is validated a third time. In Hebrews 2:2, we read:

For if the word spoken through angels proved stedfast, and every transgression and disobedience received a just recompense of reward;

In the context, the writer of the Book of Hebrews is clearly speaking of the Mosaic Law. Once again, the New Testament validates a Jewish tradition that the law was indeed given to Moses by means of angels. It is clear, of course, from the Old Testament that the Ten Commandments were written by *the finger* of God and not by the finger of an angel, but the other commandments of the Mosaic Law were in a different category. They were mediated by means of angels.

Two things have been learned about the Law of Moses so far: first, it contains a total of 613 commandments—not merely ten; and second, it was mediated by means of angels. The remainder of the chapter concentrates on the purpose of the Law of Moses, its unity, and the fact that it has been rendered inoperative. It will then discuss the new law and look at the principle of freedom.

A. THE PURPOSES OF THE LAW OF MOSES

Biblical Christianity has not believed and does not believe that the Law of Moses was a means of salvation. This concept is rejected because it would make salvation by means of works. Salvation always was and is by grace through faith. While the content of faith has changed from age to age,

75

depending on progressive revelation, the means of salvation has never changed. The law was not given to serve as a means of salvation (Rom. 3:20, 28; Gal. 2:16; 3:11, 21). It was given to a people already *redeemed* from Egypt and not in order to redeem them. However, there were several purposes for the giving of the law. As found in both testaments, there were at least nine reasons for the Law of Moses.

The first purpose was to reveal the holiness of God and to reveal the standard of righteousness which God demanded for a proper relationship with Him (Lev. 11:44; 19:1-2, 37; 1 Pet. 1:15-16). The law itself was *holy, and righteous, and good* (Rom. 7:12).

The second purpose of the law was to provide the rule of conduct for the Old Testament saints. For example, Romans 3:28 makes it clear that no man was justified by the works of the law. The law was never a means of salvation. The law always had other purposes. In this case, it provided the rule of life for the Old Testament believer (Lev. 11:44-45; 19:2; 20:7-8, 26). For the Old Testament believer, the law was the center of his spiritual life and his delight (Ps. 119; note especially vv. 77, 97, 103-104, and 159).

The third purpose was to provide for Israel occasions for individual and corporate worship. The seven holy seasons of Israel (Lev. 23) is one example of this.

The fourth purpose was to keep the Jews a distinct people (Lev. 11:44-45; Deut. 7:6; 14:1-2). This was the specific reason for many of the laws, such as the dietary laws, clothing laws, etc. The Jews were to be distinct from all other people in a variety of ways, as in the worship habits (Lev. 1-7, 16, 23), eating habits (Lev. 11:1-47), sexual habits (Lev. 12), clothing habits (Lev. 19:19), and even the way they cut their beards (Lev. 19:27). Other passages for this point include Exodus 19:5-8 and 31:13.

The fifth purpose is stated in Ephesians 2:11-16. (...) The Law of Moses served as a middle wall of partition. The four unconditional covenants are Jewish covenants, and God's blessings, both physical and spiritual, are mediated through the four covenants, the *covenants of the promise* mentioned in verse 12. Because of the Jewish nature of these unconditional covenants, a conditional covenant was also added, the Mosaic Covenant, containing the Law of Moses, the *law of commandments* and *ordinances* of verse 15. The purpose of the law, then, was to become a *middle wall of partition* to keep Gentiles, as Gentiles, from enjoying the Jewish spiritual blessings of the unconditional covenants. Because of this purpose, Gentiles were both *alienated from the commonwealth of Israel*, and *strangers from the covenants of the promise.* The only way Gentiles could enjoy the spiritual blessings of the Jewish covenants during the period of the law was to take upon themselves the obligation of the law, undergo the rite of circumcision, and then live like every Jew had to live. Gentiles, as Gentiles, could not enjoy the Jewish spiritual blessings, only Gentiles as proselytes to Mosaic Judaism.

The sixth purpose for the Mosaic Law was to reveal sin. Three passages in Romans point this out. The first is Romans 3:19-20, where Paul emphasized that there is no justification through the law; by means of the law, no Jewish person will be justified. What is the law? Since it is not a way of justification, is it a way of salvation? The law was there to provide the knowledge of sin, to reveal exactly what sin is. The second passage is Romans 5:20: The law was given so that trespasses might be made very clear. How does one know he has sinned? He knows because the law spelled out in detail what was permitted and what was not permitted. The law with 613 commandments revealed sin. The third passage is Romans 7:7. Paul again emphasized the fact that the law was given so that sin might be made known. Paul became aware of his sinful state by looking into the law and knowing that on the basis of the law, he fell short.

The seventh purpose was to make one sin more. Romans 4:15 states:

For the law works wrath; but where there is no law, neither is there transgression.

In Romans 5:20, he adds:

And the law came in besides, that the trespass might abound; but where sin abounded, grace did abound more exceedingly:

The picture Paul gives is that the law came in to cause more sin, to actually make one sin more. How does that work? Paul explained it in Romans 4:15, 7:7-13, and I Corinthians 15:56. The latter passage reads:

The sting of death is sin; and the power of sin is the law:

Basically what Paul taught is that the sin nature needs a base of operation. Furthermore, the sin nature uses the law as a base of operation. Paul said, *...where there is no law, neither is there transgression* (Rom. 4:15). He did not mean, of course, that there was no sin before the law was given. The term "transgression" is a specific type of sin: violation of a specific command-ment. Men were sinners before the law was given, but they were not transgressors of the law until the law was given. Once the law was given, the sin nature had a base of operation, causing the individual to violate these commandments and sin all the more.

The eighth purpose was to show the sinner that there was nothing he could do on his own to please God and that he had no ability to keep the law perfectly or to attain the righteousness of the law (Rom. 7:14-25).

This led to the ninth purpose, which was to drive one to faith, according to Romans 8:1-4 and Galatians 3:24-25. The final purpose of the law was to bring one to saving faith, faith in the Messiah.

The purposes of the Law of Moses can be categorized as follows:

(1) In relation to God
   a. to reveal His holiness
   b. to reveal His righteous standards
(2) In relation to Israel
   a. to keep Israel a distinct people
   b. to provide a rule of life for the Old Testament saint
   c. to provide for individual and corporate worship
(3) In relation to Gentiles, to serve as a middle wall of partition and thus keep them strangers to the unconditional Jewish covenants so as not to partake of Jewish spiritual blessings as Gentiles, but only as proselytes to Mosaic Judaism

(4) In relation to sin
    a. to reveal and show what sin is
    b. to make one sin more
    c. to show that a man cannot attain the righteousness of the law on his own
    d. to drive one to faith[25]

B. THE UNITY OF THE LAW OF MOSES

It must be understood that the Mosaic Law is viewed by the Scriptures as a single unit. When applied to the Law of Moses, the Hebrew word *Torah,* meaning "law," is always singular, even though this law contains 613 commandments. The same is true in the New Testament of the Greek word *nomos.* The division of the Law of Moses into ceremonial, legal, and moral parts is convenient for the study of the different types of commandments contained within it, but the Scriptures themselves never divide it in this way. Neither is there any scriptural basis for separating the Ten Commandments from the whole 613 and making only those perpetual. All 613 commandments are a single unit comprising the Law of Moses.

It is this principle of the unity of the Law of Moses that lies behind the statement found in James 2:10:

For whosoever shall keep the whole law, and yet stumble in one point, he is become guilty of all.

The point is clear: A person needs only to break one of the 613 commandments to be guilty of breaking all of the Law of Moses. This can only be true if the Mosaic Law is a single unit. If it is not, the guilt lies

---

[25] The text of point A was first published in Fruchtenbaum, Arnold G. *Israelology: The Missing Link in Systematic Theology.* Tustin, CA: Ariel Ministries, 1993, pages 590-593 and is presented here with minor edits.

only in the particular commandment violated, not in the whole law. In other words, if one breaks a legal commandment, he is guilty of breaking the ceremonial and moral ones as well. The same is true of breaking a moral or ceremonial commandment. To bring the point closer to home, here is a real life example: If a person eats ham, according to the Law of Moses, he is guilty of breaking the Ten Commandments, although none of them says anything about eating ham. The law is a unit, and to break one of the 613 commandments is to *become guilty of all.*

In order to have a clear understanding of the Law of Moses and its relationship to the believer, Jew or Gentile, it is necessary to view it as the Scriptures view it: as a single unit that cannot be divided into parts that have been done away with and parts that have not. Nor can certain commandments be separated in such a way as to give them a different status than the other commandments.

C. The Law of Moses
Has Been Rendered Inoperative

The clear-cut teaching of the New Testament is that the Law of Moses has been rendered inoperative with the death of the Messiah. In other words, the law—in its totality—no longer has authority over any individual. This is evident from four lines of evidence.

1. The Law no Longer Justifies, Sanctifies, or Perfects

The first line of evidence is found in Romans 7:1-6:

>*[1]Or are ye ignorant, brethren (for I speak to men who know the law), that the law hath dominion over a man for so long time as he lives? [2]For the woman that has a husband is bound by law to the husband while he lives; but if the husband die, she is discharged from the law of the husband. [3]So then if, while the husband lives, she be joined to*

another man, she shall be called an adulteress: but if the husband die, she is free from the law, so that she is no adulteress, though she be joined to another man. ⁴Wherefore, my brethren, ye also were made dead to the law through the body of Messiah; that ye should be joined to another, even to him who was raised from the dead, that we might bring forth fruit unto God. ⁵For when we were in the flesh, the sinful passions, which were through the law, wrought in our members to bring forth fruit unto death. ⁶But now we have been discharged from the law, having died to that wherein we were held; so that we serve in newness of the spirit, and not in oldness of the letter.

When a husband dies, a wife becomes a widow and so is no longer bound to *the law of the husband* (vv. 1–3). Therefore, she is free to remarry without committing the sin of adultery; she is now "free from the law," because a death has taken place. Paul then makes the theological application (vv. 4-6). Here, again, a death has taken place, the death of the Messiah. Believers have been *made dead to the law through the body of Messiah* (v. 4). The sin nature can no longer use the law as a base of operation (v. 5). Finally, Paul states that *we have been discharged from the law* (v. 6). One is either married to the law or to the Messiah but cannot be married to both.

The second line of evidence is Romans 10:4:

For Messiah is the end of the law unto righteousness to every one that believes.

The Greek word for "end," *telos*, can mean either "termination" or "goal." However, the evidence clearly favors the meaning of "end." For example, Thayer gives the primary meaning of *telos* as:

... end, i.e. a. *termination*, the *limit* at which a thing ceases
to be, ... in the Scriptures also of a temporal end;... Christ
has brought the law to an end ...[26]

Not only does Thayer give "termination" as the primary meaning of *telos*,
he also includes Romans 10:4 as belonging to that category of usage. Nor
is "goal" listed as a secondary or even a third in priority of usage; it is
fourth on the list.

Arndt and Gingrich give the primary meaning of the verbal form as *"bring
to an end, finish, complete."*[27] The nominal *telos* is given the primary
meaning of: "end ... in the sense of *termination, cessation.*"[28] They too list
Romans 10:4 as being in this category and list the meaning of "goal" as
being third on the list.

Very clearly, Messiah *is the end of the law*, and that includes all 613
commandments; hence the law has ceased to function. There is no
justification through it.

Galatians 2:16 states:

*yet knowing that a man is not justified by the works of the law but
through faith in Yeshua Messiah, even we believed on Messiah
Yeshua, that we might be justified by faith in Messiah, and not by the
works of the law: because by the works of the law shall no flesh be
justified.*

---

[26] Grimm, Carl Ludwig Wilibald, Joseph Henry Thayer, and Christian Gottlob Wilke. *Greek-English Lexicon of the New Testament; Being Grimm's Wilke's Clavis Novi Testamenti.* Grand Rapids: Zondervan Pub. House, 1970, pp. 619-620.

[27] Bauer, Walter, F. Wilbur Gingrich, Frederick W. Danker, and Walter Bauer. *A Greek-English Lexicon of the New Testament and Other Early Christian Literature: A Translation and Adaptation of the Fourth Revised and Augmented Edition of Walter Bauer's Griechisch-Deutsches Wörterbuch zu den Schriften des Neuen Testaments und der übrigen urchristlichen Literatur.* Chicago: University of Chicago Press, 1979, p. 810.

[28] Ibid., p. 811.

Furthermore, according to Hebrews 7:19, there is no sanctification or perfection through the law:

(for the law made nothing perfect), and a bringing in thereupon of a better hope, through which we draw nigh unto God.

Thus, it should be very evident that the law has come to an end in the Messiah and cannot function in justification or sanctification. For the believer especially, it has been rendered inoperative. The remaining verses (Heb. 7:20-28) however, show that the law has ceased to function altogether.

2. A Temporary Administration

That the law was never meant to be a permanent administration is stated in Galatians 3:19:

What then is the law? It was added because of transgressions, till the seed should come to whom the promise has been made;

In the context, Paul is pointing to the Law of Moses as an addition to the Abrahamic Covenant. It was added for the purpose of making sin very clear so that all will know that they have fallen short of God's standard for righteousness. It was a temporary addition until the Seed, the Messiah, would come; now that He has come, the law is no longer the mandatory rule of life. The addition has ceased to function with the cross.

3. The New Priesthood

With the Messiah, there is a new priesthood according to the order of Melchizedek, not according to the order of Aaron. The Law of Moses provided the basis for the Levitical priesthood. Thus, a new priesthood required a new law under which it could operate. This is clear from Hebrews 7:11-12 and 18:

[11]Now if there was perfection through the Levitical priesthood (for under it has the people received the law), what further need was there that another priest should arise after the order of Melchizedek, and not be reckoned after the order of Aaron? [12]For the priesthood being changed, there is made of necessity a change also of the law.

* * *

[18]For there is a disannulling of a foregoing commandment because of its weakness and unprofitableness

The point made in Hebrews 7:11-12 is that only one type of priesthood was permitted: the Aaronic or Levitical priesthood. The Levitical priesthood could not bring perfection. This is explained in Hebrews 9 and 10, which state rather clearly that animal blood cannot bring perfection; only the Messiah's blood could do that. The Mosaic Law was the basis for the Levitical priesthood. The writer of the Book of Hebrews said that for the Levitical priesthood to be done away with and be replaced by a new priesthood, the priesthood of Melchizedek, would require a change of the law. As long as the Law of Moses was in effect, no other priesthood was valid.

Was there a change of the law? Hebrews 7:18 states that the Mosaic Law was "disannulled." And because it is no longer in effect, there is now a new priesthood after the order of Melchizedek. If the Mosaic Law were still in effect, *Yeshua* could not function as a priest. But because the Mosaic Law is no longer in effect, *Yeshua* can be a priest after the Order of Melchizedek. Consequently, the Law of Moses has been "disannulled" in favor of a new law, which is the basis for the priesthood according to the Order of Melchizedek.

Then, in Hebrews 8:13:

In that he says, A new covenant, he has made the first old. But that which is becoming old and waxes aged is nigh unto vanishing away.

This statement is made after the writer quoted the New Covenant of Jeremiah 31:31-34. The point he makes is that the Law of Moses became *old* under Jeremiah and vanished away when Messiah died.

4. The New Law

Paul writes in Ephesians 2:11-16:

> *[11]Wherefore remember, that once ye, the Gentiles in the flesh, who are called Uncircumcision by that which is called Circumcision, in the flesh, made by hands; [12]that ye were at that time separate from Messiah, alienated from the commonwealth of Israel, and strangers from the covenants of the promise, having no hope and without God in the world. [13]But now in Messiah Yeshua ye that once were far off are made nigh in the blood of Messiah. [14]For he is our peace, who made both one, and broke down the middle wall of partition, [15]having abolished in the flesh the enmity, even the law of commandments contained in ordinances; that he might create in himself of the two one new man, so making peace; [16]and might reconcile them both in one body unto God through the cross, having slain the enmity thereby:*

And Ephesians 3:6 states:

> *to wit, that the Gentiles are fellow-heirs, and fellow-members of the body, and fellow-partakers of the promise in Messiah Yeshua through the gospel,*

Basically, Paul is saying that God made certain covenants with the Jewish people. In fact, there were four unconditional, eternal covenants God made with Israel: the Abrahamic Covenant, the Land Covenant, the Davidic Covenant, and the New Covenant. All of God's blessings, both material and spiritual, are mediated by means of these four eternal and unconditional Jewish covenants. At the same time, Paul points out that

God added a fifth covenant that was temporary and conditional: the Mosaic Covenant containing the Mosaic Law.

The fourth line of evidence for the annulment of the Mosaic Law zeros right in on the part of the law that most people want to retain—the Ten Commandments. A very significant passage is II Corinthians 3:2-11:

> *²Ye are our epistle, written in our hearts, known and read of all men; ³being made manifest that ye are an epistle of Messiah, ministered by us, written not with ink, but with the Spirit of the living God; not in tables of stone, but in tables that are hearts of flesh. ⁴And such confidence have we through Messiah to God-ward: ⁵not that we are sufficient of ourselves, to account anything as from ourselves; but our sufficiency is from God; ⁶who also made us sufficient as ministers of a new covenant; not of the letter, but of the spirit: for the letter kills, but the spirit gives life. ⁷But if the ministration of death, written, and engraven on stones, came with glory, so that the children of Israel could not look stedfastly upon the face of Moses for the glory of his face; which glory was passing away: ⁸how shall not rather the ministration of the spirit be with glory? ⁹For if the ministration of condemnation has glory, much rather does the ministration of righteousness exceed in glory. ¹⁰For verily that which has been made glorious has not been made glorious in this respect, by reason of the glory that surpasses. ¹¹For if that which passes away was with glory, much more that which remains is in glory.*

First, one needs to understand what Paul is saying concerning the Law of Moses. In verse seven, it is called *the ministration of death*. In verse nine, it is called *the ministration of condemnation*. These are negative yet valid descriptions. In verses three and seven, the spotlight is on the Ten Commandments since these are the ones *engraven on stones*. The main point, then, is that the Law of Moses, especially as represented by the Ten Commandments, is a *ministration of death* and a *ministration of condemnation*. If the Ten Commandments were still in force today, this would still be true.

But they are no longer in force, for it states in verses seven and 11 that the law has "passed away." The Greek word used is *katargeo*, which means "to render inoperative." Since the emphasis in this passage is on the Ten Commandments, this means that the Ten Commandments have passed away. The thrust is very clear: The Law of Moses, and especially the Ten Commandments, is no longer in effect. In fact, the superiority of the law of the Messiah is seen by the fact that it will never be rendered inoperative.

To summarize this section, the law is a unit comprised of 613 commandments, and all of it has been rendered inoperative. There is no commandment that has continued beyond the cross of the Messiah. The law is there and can be used as a teaching tool to show God's standard of righteousness and man's sinfulness and need of substitutionary atonement. It can be used to point one to the Messiah (Gal. 3:23-25). However, it has completely ceased to function as an authority over individuals.

D. THE BELIEVER IS UNDER A NEW LAW

The Law of Moses has been disannulled or rendered inoperative, and believers are now under a new law. This new law is called *the Law of Messiah* in Galatians 6:2 and *the law of the Spirit of life* in Romans 8:2. This brand-new law is totally separate from the Law of Moses. The law of the Messiah contains all the commandments applicable to a New Testament believer.

The reason there is so much confusion over the relationship between the Law of Moses and the Law of the Messiah is that many commandments are the same or similar to those found in the Mosaic Law, and many believers have concluded that certain sections of the law have therefore been retained. But it has already been shown that this cannot be the case, and the explanation for the sameness of the commandments is to be found elsewhere.

This explanation can best be understood if it is realized that there are a number of codes in the Bible such as the Edenic, Adamic, Noahic, Mosaic, and Messianic law codes. A new code will always contain some of the same commandments of the previous code, but this does not mean that the previous code is still in effect. While certain commandments of the Adamic code were also found in the Edenic code, this did not mean that it was still partially in force. The Edenic code ceased to function with the fall of man. The same is true when we compare the law of the Messiah with the Law of Moses. There are many similar commandments. For example, nine of the Ten Commandments are to be found in the law of the Messiah, but this does not mean that the Law of Moses is still in force.

Let me illustrate this by using an example many others have experienced. I received my first driver's license in the State of California, and, as long as I drove in California, I was subject to the traffic laws of that state. But after a couple of years, I moved to New York. Once I left California, I ceased to be under California traffic law. The traffic laws of that state were rendered inoperative in my case. Now my driving was subject to a new law—the traffic laws of the State of New York. Both states required me to stop at a red light. But this did not mean that New York borrowed the law from California or California from New York. Both states had their own legislature who passed the same laws. There were many laws that were different. For example, in California I was permitted to make a right turn at a red light after stopping and yielding the right-of-way, but in New York, no right turn was permitted at a red light at that time (the law has changed since then). There were many similar laws between the two states, such as the law demanding that I stop at a red light. When I stopped at a red light, I did not do so in obedience to the State of California as I once had, but in obedience to the State of New York. I proceeded at a green light, not because of California law, but because of New York law. If I went through a red light without stopping, I was not guilty of breaking California law, but New York law. Many laws were similar, but they were under two distinctly different systems.

The Law of Moses has been nullified, and believers are now under the law of the Messiah. There are many different commandments. Under the Law of Moses, one would not be permitted to eat pork, but under the law of the Messiah, he may. There are many similar commandments, but they are nonetheless in two separate systems. Therefore, if one does not kill or steal, this is not because of the Law of Moses but because of the law of the Messiah. On the other hand, if one does steal, he is not guilty of breaking the Law of Moses, but of breaking the law of the Messiah.

This understanding can solve many problems among fundamental believers, such as the issues of women wearing pants, the Sabbath, and tithing. If the commandments concerning these things are based only on the Law of Moses and not on the law of the Messiah, then they have no validity for the New Testament believer.

E. THE PRINCIPLE OF FREEDOM

This chapter has shown that the believer in the Messiah is free from the Law of Moses. This means that he is free from the necessity of keeping any commandment of that system. But on the other hand, he is also free to keep parts of the Law of Moses if he so desires, as long as it does not contradict the law of the Messiah.

The biblical basis for this freedom to keep the law can be seen in the actions of Paul, the greatest exponent of freedom from the law. His vow in Acts 18:18 is based on Numbers 6:2, 5, 9, and 18. His desire to be in Jerusalem for Pentecost in Acts 20:16 is based on Deuteronomy 16:16. The strongest passage is Acts 21:17-26, where Paul, the apostle of freedom from the law, is seen keeping the law himself. The believer is free from the Law of Moses, but he is also free to keep parts of it. Thus, if a Jewish believer feels the need to refrain from eating pork, he is free to do so. The same is true for all the other commandments.

However, there are two dangers that must be avoided by the believer who voluntarily keeps the commandments of the Law of Moses. One danger is the idea that by doing so he is contributing to his own justification and sanctification. This is false and should be avoided. The second danger is in expecting others to keep the same commandments that he had decided to keep. This is equally wrong and borders on legalism. The one who exercises his freedom to keep the law must recognize and respect another's freedom not to keep it. For Messianic Jewish believers, it must also be understood that choosing to keep parts of the Law of Moses does not add to their Jewish identity. Jewishness is not based on the Mosaic Law, but on the Abrahamic Covenant.

Chapter V –
Other False Additions to Salvation

Keeping the Law of Moses as a means of justification or sanctification and encouraging others to do the same is certainly the biggest temptation—especially for messianic believers today. But throughout Church history, various other false ideas have been added to the biblical concept of salvation. We will discuss five of them.

A. REPENTANCE

The first false addition to salvation is repentance. Some groups claim that not only does one have to believe on the Messiah and trust Him for one's salvation, one must also repent. Usually what they mean by repentance is that "one must truly be sorry for his sins." The actual meaning of the Greek word, though, is simply "to change one's mind." That is all that biblical repentance means.

When the term "repentance" is used as a synonym for faith, then yes, it is a condition for salvation. For example, one has to change one's mind about who the Messiah is in order to be saved. So if repentance is meant as a synonym for belief, then yes, repentance is necessary for salvation.

Repentance also becomes a false addition when it is taken to mean "sorrow." If by repentance one means "sorrow" and, therefore, one has to feel sorry for his sins to be saved, then it is a false addition to salvation. The reason for this is that if repentance—in the sense of being sorry for one's sins—is necessary, salvation then becomes two things. First, salvation is now placed on the basis of works, and second, salvation is based upon feeling, not upon the facts and promises of Scripture.

In salvation, repentance is never a separate act from faith or believing. Faith as a condition to salvation appears about two hundred times, and repentance as a synonym for believing is given 35 times. Only as a synonym for believing is it a condition for salvation. But if one redefines repentance as "being sorry for one's sins," then it is a false addition.

The New Testament uses the word "repentance" in four different ways. First, it is used as a synonym for believing and means nothing different than believing in *Yeshua* the Messiah. One changes his mind and believes on Him (Lk. 24:47; Acts 17:30; Rom. 2:4; II Tim. 2:25; II Pet. 3:9).

A second way that "repentance" is used is to change one's mind about anything. Again, it never carries the sense of feeling sorry. Sorrow may accompany repentance, but the word itself does not mean "sorrow." It simply means "to change one's mind" (Acts 8:22; 11:18; 20:21; 26:20; Heb. 6:1, 6; 12:17; Rev. 9:20).

A third way the word is used is in reference to Israel when speaking of Israel's need to repent, that is, Israel's need to change its mind about *Yeshua*. Here again, it merely means "a change of mind concerning who the Messiah is" (Acts 2:38; 3:19; 5:31).

A fourth way the word "repentance" is used is in reference to John's baptism, which was called a "baptism of repentance." In this sense, it is simply a part of God's covenantal relationship with Israel (Acts 13:24; 19:4).

Insofar as repentance is concerned, there are two things to note. If repentance is used merely as a synonym for believing in the Messiah—the way the Bible uses it—only in that sense is it truly a condition for salvation. But if—as some groups use it—repentance means "to feel sorry for one's sins," then it indeed becomes a false addition to salvation.

B. CONFESSION OF THE MESSIAH

Some circles teach that there must be a public confession of the Messiah for one's salvation. This "confession of the Messiah" is another false addition to salvation. This teaching is based upon two passages. First is Matthew 10:32:

Every one therefore who shall confess me before men, him will I also confess before my Father who is in heaven.

The second passage is Romans 10:9-10:

⁹because if you shall confess with your mouth Yeshua as Lord, and shall believe in your heart that God raised him from the dead, you shall be saved: ¹⁰for with the heart man believes unto righteousness; and with the mouth confession is made unto salvation.

Based upon these two passages of Scripture, some groups have made a false addition to salvation and teach that there must be a public, verbal confession for a person to be saved.

The answer is that in both of these passages, confession is not a separate act from faith. In the case of Matthew 10:32, the context is dealing with Israel's rejection of the Messiah, and those individual Jews who want salvation must *confess Yeshua* as Messiah. But in this case, the word "confession" is simply part of the act of faith; it is not a separate act in any way.

As far as the Romans 10:9-10 passage is concerned, Paul uses a Hebraic poetical form known as "inversion." He interchanges the terms "confession" and "believing" to show that these terms are used synonymously. For example, in verse nine, he first speaks of confession: *confess with your mouth Yeshua as Lord,* and then second: *believe in your heart that God raised him from the dead.* So in this verse, there is confession followed by believing. Then in verse ten, he reverses the terms. He first speaks of believing: *for with the heart man believes unto righteousness,* then he mentions confession: *with the mouth confession is made unto salvation.*

This inversion of confession and believing and the interchangeableness of the two terms show that the apostle used them synonymously. Confession in this verse equals calling upon the name of the Lord. Calling upon the name of the Lord is simply exercising faith in Him. Confession is not a separate act from faith and is made to God and not to a public audience.

There are three problems with this false addition to salvation. The first problem is that confession is omitted in all passages that speak of a condition of salvation with these two exceptions. In the other two hundred-plus cases where the condition is given for salvation, confession is not one of them. Even in these two cases, confession is used only synonymously with believing in the Messiah.

The second problem is that if a public confession were necessary for salvation, then salvation is on the basis of works.

The third problem is that the circumstances for many people who are saved preclude a public confession. Many people are saved by reading a gospel tract or the New Testament. They believe on *Yeshua* the Messiah, and they indeed experience salvation without having any opportunity to make a public confession right then and there.

A public confession is not part of salvation, and those who teach it make it a false addition to salvation.

C. CONFESSION OF SIN

Another false addition to salvation is the confession of sin. The verse which is used to validate this addition is I John 1:9:

If we confess our sins, he is faithful and righteous to forgive us our sins, and to cleanse us from all unrighteousness.

People sometimes use this verse and make it a condition of salvation by saying that one must confess his sins before he can be saved.

There are two problems with this interpretation. First of all, I John 1:9 is not a salvation verse. In fact, the writer is addressing those who already are believers; they have already been saved. Notice the pronouns: *If we confess our sins*. The pronouns *we* and *our* include the Apostle John and his readers. Both John and his readers were already saved. This is not a salvation verse; it is simply a verse which deals with the sins committed by people who already are believers.

Second, if the confession of sin were a necessary addition to salvation, the question would arise as to how many people actually remember every sin they ever committed. It would literally be impossible to remember every sin that one has committed. If this condition were true, it would mean that unless one has confessed every single sin ever committed, one cannot be saved! Since this is impossible, no one would have hope of salvation.

D. IMPLORING GOD FOR SALVATION

Yet another group of people falsely teaches that one must implore God to save him or he will not be saved. The picture is that God is somewhat reluctant to give salvation and, therefore, one must implore Him before one may receive it. Two main passages are used to teach this. First is Isaiah 55:6:

> *Seek ye Jehovah while he may be found; call ye upon him while he is near:*

The admonition to *seek ye Jehovah* is interpreted as "imploring God to save." While the admonition is to *seek* the Lord, they ignore the fact that Romans 3:11 teaches that no one seeks God on his own. If this were a condition of salvation, it would mean that no one would be saved, since no one will ever seek God on his own!

Another passage used is Luke 18:13, which speaks of praying for mercy or propitiation. What is ignored here is that this passage does not actually say that one must implore God to be saved, nor does it teach that one must seek God and seek God and seek God until one finds Him. The passage is dealing with the believer's prayer life and confession, not with salvation. Luke 19:10 states that it is the Messiah who actually does the seeking: *For the Son of man came to seek and to save that which was lost.*

The problem with this teaching is that in the two hundred-plus places where the condition for salvation is discussed, imploring God is not a condition for salvation. It is never written that one must implore, seek, and pray for God to save him before God will do it. Furthermore, this is salvation by works. The Scriptures emphazise that salvation is by grace through faith. The salvation which God offers is simply received by faith; one does not have to implore God to save him. God is more than ready to do so. If one must implore God first, then salvation is by works.

E. BAPTISM

Is baptism necessary for salvation? Some groups teach the doctrine of baptismal regeneration: that one must be baptized to be saved. Several answers can be given.

In more than two hundred passages where salvation is mentioned, faith is the only condition for salvation. If baptism were necessary for salvation, it should have been mentioned in all cases where the condition for salvation is clearly stated.

Paul did not consider baptism to be that vital. In I Corinthians 1:14-17, the apostle mentioned how happy he was that he did not baptize too many people in the Corinthian Church, thus eliminating the chance that they would count on the fact that they were baptized by Paul. Furthermore, in verse 17, he said that God did not send him to baptize, but to preach the gospel. If baptism were necessary for salvation, then Paul would have said that he was sent to preach the gospel and to baptize. When he discussed the gospel in I Corinthians 15:1-4, he pointed out that it is the gospel that saves (v. 2), and baptism is not part of that gospel.

Nevertheless, there are some "problem passages" that people use to support the doctrine of baptismal regeneration. The first one is Mark 16:16:

He that believes and is baptized shall be saved; but he that disbelieves shall be condemned.

Two things can be noted here. First, there is a real question as to whether this verse in Mark 16 was originally part of the Gospel of Mark, because the oldest and best manuscripts do not even have this passage. It is foolish to base a doctrine on a passage that is not found in the best and oldest manuscripts. Furthermore, in Matthew's parallel account (28:16-20), the statement does not exist. Baptism is a matter of discipleship, not evangelism.

A second way of answering this is to point out that it is not stated negatively. He does not say that if you do not believe and are not baptized, you will be lost. He simply says that if you do not believe, you will be lost. If baptism were necessary, he would have also said that if you believe but are not baptized, you will still be lost. He mentioned believing and baptism together because in those days, baptism immediately followed believing. In those days, people understood that the act of baptism identified them with a message, person, or group. Today, there is so much confusion concerning baptism that it might be wise to delay the baptism of the new believer until he has had a chance to be taught what baptism means.

The second passage that causes some to stumble is John 3:5:

Jesus answered, Verily, verily, I say unto you, Except one be born of water and the Spirit, he cannot enter into the kingdom of God.

This passage speaks of being *born of water*, not baptism. If it were, *Yeshua* would have used the word for baptism. Being *born of water* was a Jewish expression meaning "physical birth." "Mere physical birth as a Jew," He tells Nicodemus, "is not sufficient to enter the Kingdom." For the Kingdom, one must be born of the *Spirit*. Being *born of water* precedes being born of the *Spirit*, but in Scripture, one is not baptized before, but after believing. But the word for baptism is not used, and being *born of water* is physical birth which always precedes spiritual rebirth. In fact, the very next verse makes that distinction. Being *born of water* corresponds to being *born of the flesh*; being *born of the Spirit is spirit* corresponds to spiritual rebirth (John 3:5-6).

A third passage that leads to confusion is found in Acts 2:38:

And Peter said unto them, Repent ye, and be baptized every one of you in the name of Yeshua Messiah unto the remission of your sins; and ye shall receive the gift of the Holy Spirit.

The Greek word for *unto* in *unto the remission of your sins* is *eis*. This word is also used in Matthew 12:41, where it means "on account of." In this verse, the word *eis* should also read "on account of." Therefore, he is saying: "Repent and be baptized on account of or on the basis of the remission of sin."

Acts 22:16 is another verse we need to examine:

And now why tarries you? arise, and be baptized, and wash away your sins, calling on his name.

There are two parts to this verse that should be kept distinct. In the first part, *arise* is a participle and *be baptized* is an imperative; the word *and* is not part of the Greek text. It simply says, "arising, be baptized." In the second part, *wash away your sins* is an imperative followed by the participle *calling*. Therefore, this verse is saying that baptism follows the arising, just as forgiveness follows the calling upon the name of the Lord. One is saved by merely calling upon the name of the Lord. But after being saved by calling upon His name, he then should arise and be baptized as an act of obedience.

The last passage to consider is I Peter 3:20-21:

[20]that aforetime were disobedient, when the longsuffering of God waited in the days of Noah, while the ark was a preparing, wherein

few, that is, eight souls, were saved through water: [21]*which also after a true likeness does now save you, even baptism, not the putting away of the filth of the flesh, but the interrogation of a good conscience toward God, through the resurrection of Yeshua Messiah;*

These verses speak of a cleansing of the conscience, not salvation. These were Jewish believers who had not undergone water baptism and were operating under a bad conscience because they were disobeying the Lord. The writer is telling them that they need to have that bad conscience cleansed. The conscience is always cleansed the same way: by obeying the Lord in whatever area one is disobedient. In this case, they were in disobedience as to the command of baptism. While baptism is a symbol and a sign of cleansing, it is never the means of cleansing. Baptism is only necessary for discipleship and obedience, not for salvation. One can be a believer in *Yeshua*, but he cannot be a disciple if he has not undergone water baptism. Therefore, baptism is a false addition to the condition of salvation.

From a messianic Jewish perspective, there is another way to understand what is going on. The passages used to support that baptism is essential to salvation (Acts 2:38; 22:16; I Pet. 3:21) are all addressed to Jewish audiences, and more specifically, to the very generation guilty of the unpardonable sin and facing the judgment of A.D. 70. It should also be kept in mind that the term *salvation* is not always soteriological; depending on the context, it might be either physical or spiritual.

In Matthew 12, the leadership of Israel publically rejected the Messiahship of *Yeshua* and explained away His unique abilities to perform miracles never done before on the basis that He was possessed by the prince of demons, Beelzebub. That was when *Yeshua* withdrew the offer of the Messianic Kingdom and declared that that generation was guilty of the unpardonable sin, the blasphemy of the Holy Spirit. This was a national sin, not an individual one, and it was limited to the Jewish generation of *Yeshua's* day and not applicable to all subsequent Jewish generations (a common fallacy of all forms of Replacement Theology). He also declared the coming physical judgment upon that generation which was fulfilled when the Romans destroyed Jerusalem and the Second Temple and forced the Jewish people into dispersion in A.D. 70.

However, the unpardonable sin was a national sin, not an individual sin. Individual members of that generation could and did escape that judgment, but they would need to do the two things of Acts 2:38. First, they would need to repent, a term that means a change of mind. They would need to change their mind about *Yeshua*, that He was not demonized, but that He was the Messiah, and that alone would save them spiritually. But it would not save them physically from the A.D. 70 judgment. Therefore, the second thing they would have to do is to separate themselves from that generation guilty of the unpardonable sin, and that separation would save them physically. This is obvious from verse forty when Peter admonishes them to *save yourselves from this crooked generation*. It is obvious they could not save themselves spiritually since only God can do that and will do so by grace through faith. But they could save themselves physically by separating themselves from *this crooked generation,* and that will come by means of water baptism. Thus, in verse 41, they underwent baptism.

In these passages, baptism will save the Jewish believers of *that generation* physically, but faith alone will save them spiritually.

F. THE LORDSHIP OF MESSIAH

The last false addition to salvation we will look at is called Lordship salvation. This view states that one must not only accept *Yeshua* as one's Savior or Messiah, but also accept Him as Lord of one's life; only then one can be saved.

1. The Theology of Lordship

In order to understand what is meant by Lordship salvation or the Lordship of Messiah, we need to discuss four specific terms. Then we will look at the content of the teaching and how it relates to salvation.

a. The Meaning of the Terms

(1) Jehovah

First and foremost is the term "Jehovah". In Hebrew that name is comprised of four letters, which correspond to the English letters *YHVH* (or *YHWH*). In most English translations, this name of God is translated as LORD, with all four letters capitalized. In others, the word Jehovah is used. This name for God, LORD or Jehovah, is used in the Hebrew Bible a total of 6,832 times and has five specific aspects:

1. The root meaning of *YHVH* is "to be." It emphasizes God as the eternal, self-existing One (Ex. 3:14).
2. The name emphasizes God as a covenant-keeper especially in His relationship to Israel, because God is related to Israel by covenant (Gen. 15:12-21).
3. It emphasizes God as the unchanging One (Mal. 3:6).
4. It emphasizes God's righteousness and *YHVH* as the Judge because of His righteousness (Gen. 18:25-26; Ps. 11:4-6).
5. It emphasizes God's love in that, as *YHVH*, He is both the Redeemer and Savior of the sinner (Is. 63:7-9; Jer. 31:1-6). This is a product of *YHVH's* love.

(2) Adon

The second specific term used in the context of Lordship salvation is the Hebrew word *Adon,* which is translated three ways in English Bibles: "master;" "lord," when used of a human being; and "Lord," with a capital "L," when used of God. Whereas YHVH or Jehovah is translated with all four letters capitalized (LORD), *Adon* is translated with only the first letter capitalized (Lord).

The word *Adon* is used of both God and man. It is used of man more than three hundred different times in the Hebrew Bible and has seven different aspects:

1. *Adon* is used of a man as being the lord of his wife (Gen. 18:12).
2. It is used as a polite address, like the Old English *my lord* (Gen. 23:6).
3. It is used for the lord of a slave (Gen. 24:12).
4. It is used for the lord of property (Gen. 42:30).
5. It is used for the lord of the house (Gen. 45:8).
6. It is used as a title of veneration (Num. 11:28).
7. It is used as a royal court term (I Sam. 26:17).

However, it is also used of God, and thirty times it is used in conjunction with the term Jehovah or YHVH, emphasizing His special Lordship (Ex. 34:23; Deut. 10:17; Ps. 97:5; 114:7; 135:5; 136:1-3; Is. 1:24; 3:1; 10:16, 33; 19:4; Mic. 4:13; Zech. 6:5). These usages of *Adon* in conjunction with *YHVH* show five different aspects of meaning:

1. *Adon* emphasizes God as master.
2. It emphasizes God as Lord.
3. It emphasizes God as sovereign.
4. It emphasizes that God is owner of this world.
5. It emphasizes that God is the One in control of this world.

(3) *Adonai*

The third specific term is the Hebrew word *Adonai*. It is the plural form of *Adon*, meaning "my Lords." Whereas the singular *Adon* is used of both God and man, the plural *Adonai* is used only of God. The term emphasizes God as master.

It appears a total of 449 times: 135 times it is used all by itself; 315 times it is found in conjunction with the name *YHVH*—310 times it is *Adonai* Jehovah and five times *YHVH Adonai*.

These usages have three different aspects:

1. The *fear of the Lord* is the source of wisdom (Job 28:28).
2. It emphasizes God's ownership of the world (Ps. 8:1-9).
3. It emphasizes His claim of absolute obedience (Mal. 1:6).

By way of application to Lordship concepts, the name *YHVH* emphasizes our dependence upon this Lord, and the term *Adonai* emphasizes the obedience that this Lord requires from us.

(4) *Kurios*

The fourth specific term is the one main Greek term used: *Kurios*. In Classical Greek, it was used in three ways:

1. To emphasize someone as being an owner
2. As one being in full authority
3. As one who has lawful power of disposal

Kurios is never used of the Greek gods. In the Septuagint, it is used as the Greek equivalent to *YHVH* 6,156 times of the 6,832 times that *YHVH* appears. It is also used to translate the terms *Adon* and *Adonai*. *Kurios* is used for both God and man, and it is also used of another Hebrew term, *baal*, emphasizing ownership. The New Testament follows both the Classical and Septuagint usages; it expresses the ideas of obedience and submission, and it is the address of respect. It is used of the ownership of an animal (Lk. 19:33) and ownership of a slave (Lk. 16:3; Mat. 13:27; 25:26; Acts 16:16-19). It is used as a court term (Mat. 27:62-63) and of a husband as the lord of his wife (I Pet. 3:6).

b. *The Lordship of the Messiah*

Concerning the Lordship of the Messiah per se, we should note that *Yeshua* is Lord in both Testaments.

In the Old Testament, it is God who refers to Himself as the *I AM*. In the New Testament, *Yeshua* calls Himself by the same name. (Jn. 8:58; 18:5-6)

Many *YHVH* passages in the Old Testament are applied to *Yeshua* in the New Testament. For example, in Psalm 102:12, God is addressed as *YHVH*. Verses 25-27 of the same psalm elaborate on who He is. They are quoted in the New Testament in Hebrews 1:10-12 and are applied to the Messiah. Another example is Isaiah 6:5, where, again, God is addressed as

YHVH; John 12:41 applies that verse to *Yeshua*. It is clear that *YHVH* in the Old Testament is often the same as *Yeshua* in the New Testament.

Furthermore, the Old Testament Hebrew terms *Adon* and *Adonai* are also applied to *Yeshua* in the New Testament. For example, in Deuteronomy 10:17, God is addressed as *Adon* or *Adonai*, and this verse is quoted and applied to *Yeshua* in I Timothy 6:13-15. Isaiah 6:1 and 8-10 are applied to *Yeshua* in John 12:39-40. Isaiah 53:1 is applied to *Yeshua* in John 12:38. Psalm 110:1 uses the term *Adon*, which is applied to *Yeshua* several times in the New Testament (Mat. 22:41-45; Mk. 12:35-37; Lk. 20:41-44; Acts 2:34-36; Heb. 1:13). Clearly, then, *Yeshua* is the Lord of the Old Testament.

But He is also the Lord of the New Testament. This point concerning the Lordship of the Messiah contains twelve facets:

1. The Greek term *Kurios* is the Greek word that corresponds to *YHVH*, *Adon*, and *Adonai* in the Old Testament. *Kurios* is applied to *Yeshua* in the New Testament in all the various shades of meaning that are found in the Old Testament. In fact, *Kurios* is used of *Yeshua* 747 times.
2. He is *Lord of all* (Acts 10:36; Rom. 10:12; Eph. 4:4-5).
3. He is the *Lord of glory* (I Cor. 2:8).
4. He is the LORD of LORDS (Rev. 17:14; 19:16).
5. Because He is Lord, all angels are in subjection to Him (I Pet. 3:22).
6. Because He is the Lord, He is the *head* of humanity (Rom. 14:9; I Cor. 11:3).
7. Because He is Lord, He exercises headship of the universe (Eph. 1:20-22).
8. Because He is Lord, He is also the *head of the church.* (Eph. 1:22-23; 5:23; Col. 1:18; 2:19).
9. Because He is the Lord, He is the *lord of the sabbath* (Mat. 12:8; Mk. 2:28).
10. He is the Messiah Lord (Mk. 1:3; Lk. 2:11; 3:4). In fact, the common rabbinic name for the Messiah was "King Messiah," and this rabbinic concept is reflected in referring to *Yeshua* as "Lord Messiah" in the New Testament.

11. He is also known as the Lord God (Jn. 20:28).
12. And He is also the Lord of the believers (Jn. 13:13-14; II Cor. 4:5; 12:8; Eph. 6:9).

Based upon the fact that He is the Lord of the Old Testament and the Lord of the New Testament, there are seven specific conclusions about the Lordship of the Messiah.

First, He is the Creator. In order to create, one has to be Lord. Because He is the Lord, He is also the Creator. That is why John 1:1-3 emphasizes that all things were made through Him and without Him there would be nothing that now exists, for He is the agent of creation.

Second, He is the Covenant-Keeper. The primary meaning of the term *YHVH* is to emphasize God as the Covenant-Keeper, and that is what He is. He will make sure that all God's covenants are indeed fulfilled.

Third, He is self-existent. Because another key meaning of the term "Jehovah" emphasizes God as the self-existing One, so *Yeshua* is self-existent. His existence is not dependent on any other element.

Fourth, He is Master. A master is someone who must be obeyed. The fact that He is our Master means that we must obey Him; we must render our obedience to Him.

Fifth, *Yeshua* is Owner. He is the Owner of the world because He created the world. He is the Owner of all humanity because He created all humanity. But He is also the Owner of every believer in a special way: We are a new creation in Him by virtue of regeneration. Because He is our Owner, He has the right to place us and to deal with us as He wills.

Sixth, He is the Ruler. As Lord He must be Ruler, and this points out that He is our sovereign Ruler and can do as He wills.

And seventh, He is central to everything. He is central to the universe, central to human existence, central to our faith, and central to our salvation.

c. The Relationship of Lordship to Salvation

After having studied the content of the theology of Lordship, we will now look at its relationship to salvation. The issue is this: Must there be a commitment to the Messiah as Lord of one's life in order to be saved?

Many say, "Yes, for a person to be saved he must make a commitment to the Messiah and make the Messiah Lord of his life. If he does not make the Messiah Lord of his life, then he is not saved." There are some good men who actually teach this. For example, the English evangelist and scholar, Arthur W. Pink, (1886-1952), wrote in his work *Studies on Saving Faith*:

> Those preachers who tell sinners they may be saved ... *without* surrendering to the Lordship of Christ are as erroneous and dangerous as others who insist that salvation is by works. ... In most instances the modern "evangelist" assures his congregation that *all* any sinner has to do in order to escape Hell and make sure of Heaven is to "receive Christ as personal savior." But such teaching is utterly misleading. No one can receive Christ as his Saviour while he *rejects him as Lord.* Therefore, those who have not bowed to Christ's sceptre and enthroned Him in their hearts and lives, and yet imagine that they are trusting in Him as their Saviour, *are deceived...*[29]

I might point out that those who do not believe that the Messiah must be accepted as Lord of one's life in order for one to be saved do not teach that a person can be saved by accepting *Yeshua* as Savior and rejecting Him as Lord. What they are saying is that the unbeliever does not really have that concept in mind. This will be discussed in more detail later.

Another example of those who teach Lordship salvation is from the English Christian leader and Anglican cleric, John R. Stott (1921-2011):

---

[29] Pink, Arthur Walkington. *Studies on Saving Faith*. Granbury, TX: PBM Desktop Publications, 2005, pages 6,7.

I am suggesting therefore that it is as unbiblical as it is unrealistic to divorce the Lordship from the Saviorhood of Jesus Christ.[30]

The British born Canadian theologian, J. I. Packer, writes this:

Or will it leave them supposing that all they have to do is to trust Christ as a sin-bearer, not realizing that they must also deny themselves and enthrone Him as their Lord (the error we might call only-believism)?[31]

John MacArthur, American Calvinist and Baptist, states in his book, *The Parables of the Kingdom*, that "there is a transaction made to purchase salvation, but it's not with money or good works. The transaction is this: You give up all you have for all He has."[32] He goes on to say, "You give up all that you are and receive all that He is . . . A person becomes saved when he is willing to abandon everything he has to affirm, that Christ is the Lord of his life."[33]

Perhaps the most common example of the doctrine of Lordship salvation is the *Four laws* booklet published by Campus Crusade for Christ: The fourth law says that we must individually receive *Yeshua* as Savior and Lord, then we can know and experience God's plan for our lives.

---

[30] Harrison, Everett F. & John R. Stott, "Must Christ Be Lord To Be Savior?" *Eternity* 10(9):13-18, 36-7, 48, September. 1959. p. 37.

[31] Packer, J. I. *Evangelism & the Sovereignty of God.* Downers Grove, IL: Intervarsity Press, 1961, p. 89.

[32] MacArthur, John. *The Parables of the Kingdom.* Chicago: Moody Press, 1985, p. 108.

[33] Ibid., p. 109.

(1) A Clear Definition of the Gospel

To resolve the issue of Lordship salvation, there must be a clear definition of the gospel. There are two options in dealing with the question: Is salvation by grace through faith alone, or is it faith plus the commitment of one's life to the Lordship of the Messiah? One of these two options has to be a false gospel.

In the Scriptures there are examples of uncommitted believers, people who are obviously saved but not committed. One example is in Acts 10:14, where the Apostle Peter said, *"Not so, Lord; for I have never eaten anything that is common and unclean."* Peter was a believer. He had certainly made the Messiah Lord of his life in various facets, but he had a hard time submitting to the Lordship of *Yeshua* in the issue of going to the home of a Gentile and in the issue of killing and eating unkosher or unclean things.

Another example of an uncommitted believer would be Mark who quit the first missionary journey. His disobedience led to Acts 15:39:

And there arose a sharp contention, so that they parted asunder one from the other, and Barnabas took Mark with him, and sailed away unto Cyprus; ...

Yet, as with Peter, the lack of commitment was temporary. A better example would be the converts of Ephesus in Acts 19:18-19:

[18] Many also of them that had believed came, confessing, and declaring their deeds. [19] And not a few of them that practised magical arts brought their books together and burned them in the sight of all; and they counted the price of them, and found it fifty thousand pieces of silver.

These are clearly said to be believers, but they are uncommitted believers. Their lack of submission to the Lordship of the Messiah was continual and willful, unlike Peter and Mark where the disobedience was merely temporary. There are examples in the New Testament of saved people who lacked commitment in one or more areas of their lives, where it was obvious that *Yeshua* was not the Lord of their lives.

(2) The Meaning of the Word "Lord" in Relationship to Salvation

In trying to resolve the issue, one must take into account the meaning of the word "Lord." As pointed out earlier, the term "Lord" has a number of different facets and aspects. Even if we limit the aspect of Lordship to salvation, there are variations in the concept within Scriptures. In discussing the aspect of the Lordship that saves, three things should be noted.

First of all, the expression "Lord" in the title "Lord *Yeshua*" means more than just becoming the master of one's life. It is not simply Lord *Yeshua* in the sense of "Master *Yeshua*." Rather, the term "Lord" emphasizes *Yeshua* as God, and so the term "Lord *Yeshua*" emphasizes Him as the God-Man. *Yeshua* emphasizes His humanity. Lord emphasizes His deity. So Lord *Yeshua* means He is the God-Man.

First Corinthians 12:3 states that no man can say: *Yeshua is Lord but in the Holy Spirit.* Unsaved men may say it in the sense of "master," but *Lord* also means "the sense of being God," and one can recognize the deity of *Yeshua* without being willing to make Him sovereign over a particular matter, as Peter did in Acts 10:14. One can accept *Yeshua* as God, but that does not mean he is making Him the Lord of every aspect of his life. Peter knew about the deity of the Messiah, he believed it, and he accepted it, but he failed to make Him the Lord of his life in that one area at that point of time.

Accepting the Lord *Yeshua* is to accept Him as the God-Man and not as the sovereign over every area of our lives. When the Bible says that the unbeliever must believe on the Lord *Yeshua* the Messiah, it simply means he is accepting Him as the God-Man. That is what he is believing and accepting when he is saved. He is not making Him, at that point, the sovereign over every area of his life. The issue for salvation, then, is Lord *Yeshua* as the God-Man, not Lord *Yeshua* as the Master-Man.

The second thing to note is that the Messiah must be Lord in the sense of Jehovah in order to be qualified as Savior, for only God can save.

However, His personal Lordship over the individual's life is not a condition for salvation.

The third thing to note is that the Greek term *Kurios* has the meaning of "God," which was something new with the Septuagint. As seen before, in the New Testament, the term *Kurios* is used of God, of a husband, of a master, of a Roman officer, or simply as the title "Sir." The Lordship over a believer is only one aspect of *Kurios*. This one aspect alone cannot be made a condition of salvation.

So, must the Messiah be master of every area of one's life in order that he can be saved? Is that what it means to accept *Yeshua* as Lord, or does it mean merely to accept *Yeshua* as the God-Man because He must be both God and man to qualify as Savior? There are five key passages that speak to this issue.

In Romans 1:1-4, one reads:

> *¹Paul, a servant of Yeshua Messiah, called to be an apostle, separated unto the gospel of God, ²which he promised afore through his prophets in the holy scriptures, ³concerning his Son, who was born of the seed of David according to the flesh, ⁴who was declared to be the Son of God with power, according to the spirit of holiness, by the resurrection from the dead; even Yeshua Messiah our Lord,*

In these verses, Paul clearly spells out the gospel. He points out the humanity of *Yeshua* by referring to Him as the Son of David. He also points out the deity of the Messiah by calling Him the *Son of God*. What saved the believing Romans was the fact that *Yeshua* was both God and man; His Lordship emphasized His deity, not His mastership over everyone's life. In fact, Paul does not even discuss *Yeshua* as Lord of one's life until he gets to Romans 12. But he discusses the Lordship of *Yeshua* in the sense that *Yeshua* is God, and that is what one believes when he accepts *Yeshua* as Lord—that He is the God-Man, not that He is the Lord over every individual aspect of the believers' lives.

Romans 10:9-10 speaks about confessing *Yeshua as Lord*:

⁹because if you shall confess with your mouth Yeshua as Lord, and shall believe in your heart that God raised him from the dead, you shall be saved: ¹⁰for with the heart man believes unto righteousness; and with the mouth confession is made unto salvation.

According to these verses, in order to be saved, one must confess *Yeshua as Lord*. This is not *Lord* in the sense of becoming a master in every facet of one's life, but rather *Lord* in the sense of deity. He must confess the Lordship of *Yeshua*. The term *Lord* emphasizes His deity, and the term *Yeshua* emphasizes His humanity, so what must be confessed is the God-Man for salvation. One owns Him as the God-Man in order to be saved. One does not own Him as the master of his life in order to be saved.

Acts 2:36 explains the Father's role in this:

Let all the house of Israel therefore know assuredly, that God has made him both Lord and Messiah, this Yeshua whom ye crucified.

This verse declares that the Father *made him both Lord and Messiah*. Again, the term *Lord* emphasizes the deity; the term *Messiah* emphasizes His humanity.

First Corinthians 12:3 reiterates this concept:

Wherefore I make known unto you, that no man speaking in the Spirit of God says, Yeshua is anathema; and no man can say, Yeshua is Lord, but in the Holy Spirit.

We know that people can mouth the words *Yeshua is Lord* without owning Him as the Lord God. Again, this verse emphasizes that *Yeshua* must be both God **and** man to qualify as Savior.

Philippians 2:8-11 explains what it is one must confess:

⁸and being found in fashion as a man, he humbled himself, becoming obedient even unto death, yea, the death of the cross. ⁹Wherefore also

> *God highly exalted him, and gave unto him the name which is above every name;* [10]*that in the name of Yeshua every knee should bow, of things in heaven and things on earth and things under the earth,* [11]*and that every tongue should confess that Yeshua Messiah is Lord, to the glory of God the Father.*

Here again, one must confess *Yeshua* the Messiah as Lord in the sense that He is God, not in the sense that He becomes the master of one's life at the time that he is saved.

These five passages which are often used to teach Lordship salvation do not, in fact, teach that. The aspect of Lordship that saves is His deity. Indeed, *Yeshua* must be God in order to be able to save people. When they accept Him as their Lord, at the time of salvation, they are accepting Him as God their Savior. They are not making Him Lord of their lives and committing every aspect of thier lives at that point. It requires some spiritual growth before one attains that goal.

The discussion about the relationship of Lordship to salvation will be closed by drawing an analogy. The two terms *Yeshua* and "Lord" have various facets. For instance, the name *Yeshua* points to His real humanity that died for one's sins. It emphasizes His humanity as the example of his life (I Pet. 2:21; I Jn. 2:6). It implies the Second Coming (Acts 1:11; Zech. 12:10). So the name *Yeshua* has these various aspects. Does one have to believe all these aspects in order to be saved? No, he has to believe only the first aspect to be saved: that He, as a man, died for our sins. The term "Lord" also has various aspects. It could mean "God" or "creator" or "king" or "sovereign." Does one need to believe all of these facets to be saved? Again, the answer is "no." Only the first point is necessary for salvation: to believe that He is God.

When believers own Him as Lord, they own Him as God, and that is what saves them. They do not own Him as master in every facet of their lives at the moment they believe. That is something, which may happen after salvation, but is not part of it.

2. Making the Messiah Lord of One's Life

The second major section of the Lordship of the Messiah pertains to the true meaning of making Him Lord over one's life. It has been pointed out that one is not saved by making Him Lord of one's life. One is saved by believing that He died for sins, was buried and rose again, and that He is the God-Man. This is what saves. The Bible encourages believers, as they grow, to make the Messiah the Lord of their lives. In this context, there are two major topics that need to be discussed: the issue of dedication and the issue of living a Spirit-filled life.

a. The Issue of Dedication

There is a great amount of imbalance in what believers have been taught concerning dedication. Some believe that the act of dedication is the entire answer to the spiritual life and all of its problems. In other circles, dedication has little place in the spiritual life. It is never talked about, never discussed. These are actually two extremes. One extreme makes dedication the entire answer, and the other extreme does not even deal with it. There is a third reason for the imbalance: The emphasis in some circles is on rededication. There are those who constantly harp on being rededicated and rededicated and rededicated, and so periodically a person must undergo a process of rededication.

So what, then, is the biblical role of dedication? When the Bible encourages us to dedicate our lives to God, the exhortation is always based on the blessings already granted. The chief blessing, of course, is redemption. That is the point of Romans 12:1, which is a great verse on dedication, but it is based upon the word *therefore*.

I beseech you therefore, brethren, by the mercies of God, to present your bodies a living sacrifice, holy, acceptable to God, which is your spiritual service.

The reason believers ought to dedicate their lives is because of what God has already done for them, which Paul dealt with in chapters 1-11 of the

Book of Romans. In Romans 3:24, for example, he connects justification and redemption:

being justified freely by his grace through the redemption that is in Messiah Yeshua

Because of their position in the Messiah, they have been justified through redemption, and because they have been justified through redemption, they should dedicate themselves to God.

In Romans 8:23, Paul gives another reason:

And not only so, but ourselves also, who have the first-fruits of the Spirit, even we ourselves groan within ourselves, waiting for our adoption, to wit, the redemption of our body.

Because they have the assurance of the future redemption of their bodies, believers should dedicate their lives to God.

In I Corinthians 6:19-20, Paul mentions the price of redemption:

[19]Or know ye not that your body is a temple of the Holy Spirit which is in you, which ye have from God? and ye are not your own; [20]for ye were bought with a price: glorify God therefore in your body.

Because of what it cost God to redeem them, because of the *price* of redemption, the blood of the Messiah, because of what it cost God, the death of His Son, believers should dedicate their lives to the Messiah.

Dedication is always on the basis of the blessings that have already been granted by God and on the basis of blessings which believers have already received.

(1) The Concept of Dedication

Because dedication is on the basis of redemption, it is important to understand the concept of redemption. There are three key Greek words which emphasize this concept.

The first Greek word is *agorazo*, which means "to buy" or "to purchase" or "to pay a price." In the realm of redemption, it means, "to pay the price our sins demanded so that we could be redeemed." This word is used in II Peter 2:1 and Revelation 5:9.

The second Greek word is *exagorazo*, which means, "to purchase out of the market." In the area of redemption, it emphasizes the fact that the blood of the Messiah removed believers from the marketplace of sin in order to give them assurance that they will never need to go back to the slavery of sin. This word is used in Galatians 3:13 and 4:5.

The third Greek word is *lutreo*, which means, "to release and set free." In the area of redemption, it means that "the purchased person has been set free." It is used in Matthew 20:28 and Titus 2:14.

These Greek words emphasize redemption. Redemption is the basis of why believers should dedicate their lives to the Messiah and make Him the Lord of their lives in every facet.

Based upon these three Greek words, six conclusions can be drawn:

1. The redeemed person is purchased, removed from the marketplace, released, and set free.
2. This does not mean he turns from the slavery of sin to the slavery of the Messiah; that is not automatic. He is no longer a slave to sin, but that does not mean he is automatically a slave to the Messiah.
3. It means he moves from slavery to freedom.
4. So he now has a choice: He can choose to become a slave of the Messiah or he can choose not to become a slave of the Messiah.
5. Why should he choose to become a slave of the Messiah? After all, he has been saved, he is assured of Heaven, and he will not lose his salvation. So why bother becoming a slave of the Messiah? The reason is because of what the Messiah did: He provided justification, sanctification, and glorification. Deuteronomy 15:16-17 discusses the freed slave. A slave who has been freed may choose to become a slave again. If he becomes a slave again, it is because he loves his master and because the master has been good to him. He moves from being a slave to being a bond-slave and now has the right of special provisions, according to Exodus 12:43-45 and Leviticus 22:10-11.

6. Dedication is urged upon the believer on the basis of his redemption. He has been purchased, he has been removed, and he has been released. He should now dedicate his life because *Yeshua* has been good to him and because he loves Him.

(2) The Content of Dedication

When the Bible encourages believers to dedicate, what does it want them to dedicate? Three key passages are relevant.

The first passage is Romans 6:12-13:

> [12]*Let not sin therefore reign in your mortal body, that ye should obey the lusts thereof:* [13]*neither present your members unto sin as instruments of unrighteousness; but present yourselves unto God, as alive from the dead, and your members as instruments of righteousness unto God.*

The second key passage is Romans 12:1-2:

> [1]*I beseech you therefore, brethren, by the mercies of God, to present your bodies a living sacrifice, holy, acceptable to God, which is your spiritual service.* [2]*And be not fashioned according to this world: but be ye transformed by the renewing of your mind, that ye may prove what is the good and acceptable and perfect will of God.*

The third passage is I Corinthians 6:19-20:

> [19]*Or know ye not that your body is a temple of the Holy Spirit which is in you, which ye have from God? and ye are not your own;* [20]*for ye were bought with a price: glorify God therefore in your body.*

According to these three passages, what is to be dedicated is the *body*, the person himself. What God wants a believer to dedicate for His use is himself, especially his instruments, his physical instruments, his physical body. That becomes the area of dedication. That is the content of dedication. That is the subject of dedication.

In light of that, what is the relationship between salvation and dedication? Some people confuse the two. Sometimes Romans 12:1 is taught as if it were a salvation verse. As far as salvation is concerned, salvation relates to *Yeshua* the Messiah as the substitute for sin; salvation involves the sin question. However, dedication relates to the Messiah as the Lord of one's life; dedication involves subjection. Dedication, therefore, is something that follows salvation. It is not the cause or means of salvation.

The main issue in the area of dedication is: who will control one's life? Dedication does not deal with the specifics, such as, what mission field he should go to, what Bible school he should attend, whom he should marry. Dedication does not deal with these specific things. The main issue in dedication is: Who is going to control the believer's life, God or self? The issue in dedication is not yielding something, but yielding someone. And it is the believer, his body, which God wants to have dedicated to His service.

The conclusion concerning the content of dedication is this: The area of dedication is one's life and one's body. This, of course, includes the details of life, not as a means of dedication, but rather as a result of dedication. If a believer commis himself, if he dedicates himself and his whole body to God's use, these details will naturally be involved as well. But the details are the result of dedication, not the means of dedication.

(3) The Aspects of Dedication

The aspects of dedication can be summarized as an initial act of dedication and then a continuous commitment to it. The main passage dealing with this is Romans 12:1-2, quoted on page 116.

First, there must be an initial act of dedication. There must be a decisive presentation of the body to God's use. The Greek form of the word *present* is the aorist infinitive. The aorist emphasizes a single act, not repeated actions as does the present tense. The same tense is used in Romans 6:13, where it is the aorist imperative.

Believers should make a singular, decisive dedication of their bodies to God's use. Paul points out that this is a reasonable, rational, and logical thing to do in light of *the mercies of God*, which they have received in salvation. Dedication is always based on previous blessings of God, and Paul spelled out these blessings in Romans 1-11, where he pointed out that God has provided a salvation that includes justification, sanctification, and glorification. In light of all that God has done for them, in light of *the mercies of God*, which they have received in their salvation, it is a reasonable, rational, and logical thing to do.

He also points out that this is a sacrificial thing. They are to live for the Messiah in the daily routine of life now. They are sacrificing their bodies to His use. Furthermore, this should be *a living sacrifice*, not a dead one. It is to be a total and complete presentation.

The second aspect of dedication is nonconformity. This involves a separation from or nonconformity to the evil age in which we live. That is the point of Romans 12:2 and Galatians 1:4. This is the negative aspect of dedication; it involves the outward. Conformity means that the outward appearance is similar to the world, although inwardly a transformation has taken place. Non-conformity means "to be unfashionable," and that is also the point of I Peter 1:14. A life of nonconformity, although it is unfashionable, is a necessary characteristic of a dedicated life.

The third aspect is transformation. This is the positive side of dedication; it involves the inward. According to II Corinthians 3:18, the means of the transformation is the Holy Spirit. The center is the mind, and it becomes a matter of reprogramming our mind. The Holy Spirit is doing this to get believers to think the way God thinks.

(4) The Frequency of Dedication

In many circles, there is an emphasis on continuous rededication; so almost every summer at Christian camps, conferences, and bonfires, people share testimonies and talk about how they have rededicated their lives. They seem to need to do this periodically, at least once a year.

Actually, the Bible does not teach continuous rededications. The key verse on dedication is Romans 12:1, emphasizing a one-time act. When the believer has made this one-time act of Romans 12:1, and he has once-and-for-all dedicated his life for His service, he has a dedicated life. There is no need to rededicate his life. At that point, the life has been dedicated. When one comes to a crossroads in life, the issue is not: Will he do the will of God? Rather, the issue is: What is the will of God? Then, knowing the will of God, he does it.

Let's suppose a believer has made this initial, one-time act of complete dedication. After he has made it, at some point, he is faced with a life choice. Unfortunately, he makes the wrong choice and chooses not to do the will of God. The question arises: What is his status? Does he now have to rededicate his life? Obviously, his status is that he has gone back on the vow that he made when he dedicated his body for the Lord's use. Sin has now entered his life and the dedication status has been violated.

What is the remedy? The remedy is not rededication, where the believer has to start the dedicated life all over again. The remedy is restoration. The remedy is getting back on the right track. In other words, when he made that once-and-for-all act of dedication, he started on the road of a dedicated life, but, when he went back on his vow, he got off the track. The remedy is to get back on the track from where he left off. He does not have to go all the way back to the beginning and start the process all over again. He needs to get back on the track at the point where he got off. He does not have to go back to point A. If he, in a dedicated life, went from point A to B to C, but when he got to D, he fell off the track, the issue is to get back on the track at point D and continue on in the spiritual life. That is the remedy. That is restoration. The remedy is not rededication; the remedy is restoration.

The means of restoration is the confession of I John 1:9:

If we confess our sins, he is faithful and righteous to forgive us our sins, and to cleanse us from all unrighteousness.

The result is going to be restoration of fellowship. So that is the remedy: Restoration is by means of confession.

Every believer is either on one side of the line of dedication or on the other side. Either he has made the commitment or he has not made the commitment. If one has never made the dedication of Romans 12:1, this is his next step. He needs to study Romans 1-11, learn what God has done for him, and realize all the blessings of *the mercies of God* which he has received. Once he realizes this, then he applies Romans 12:1, and he makes that decisive, initial act of dedication. Again, every believer is either on one side or the other of the line of dedication. Either he has dedicated his body or he has not dedicated his body. If he has not, his next step in the spiritual life is to make that act of dedication.

Having made it, the believer begins growing in the spiritual life. If somewhere along the line he slips, he does not have to rededicate his life; rather, he needs to confess his sin and get back on track, pressing on to spiritual maturity.

Have **you** made that act of dedication? If the answer is "no," this is your next step. If the answer is "yes," then it is always profitable to examine the present state of the dedicated life: Where are we in relation to the dedication that we already made? Are we still living consistently with it or not? If we are no longer living consistently with the dedication, then the step we need to follow is to confess and get back on track. It is restoration, not rededication.

(5) The Results of Dedication

Proper biblical dedication will lead to two results. First, Romans 12:2 brings in the knowledge, the doing, and the enjoying of the will of God.

It is hard to understand what the will of God is without this act of dedication because the believer does not have the Spirit's illumination, which is needed to determine God's will from His Word. Dedication brings knowledge of the will of God. Having the knowledge, the logical outworking of the dedicated life is that the believer now does the will of God. And then doing the will of God means the enjoyment of God's will. There is really great pleasure to be derived from doing the will of God.

The second result is that it leads to a Spirit-filled life, or a Spirit-controlled life, which will be discussed in more detail in the next section.

This initial act of dedication is the starting point for victory in the spiritual life. Without it, the believer will not have consistent victory in his spiritual life. However, with it, he has the basis and the foundation for victory. When he makes Him the Lord of his life, God becomes his Master, and he becomes His slave. As the Master, God has the right to expect obedience, but as His slave, the believer has the right to expect Him to provide the power for it. And this He does, according to Philippians 4:19.

b. The Issue of Living a Spirit-Filled Life

The second major topic involved in making the Messiah Lord of one's life has to do with that which follows dedication: the Spirit-filled life.

While dedication is a once-and-for-all act which the believer performs, the Spirit-filled life is something he does in daily living. Consequently, the ministries of the Holy Spirit in relation to salvation, too, are once-and-for-all acts. These are things He does once He is in the believer's life at the time of salvation, and these acts are not repeated. There are five such ministries of the Spirit.

The first ministry is the work of **conviction**, in which He makes the gospel very clear so that it is understood by the mind of man (Jn. 16:7-11).

The second ministry is the work of **regeneration**. Regeneration causes the one who believes to be born again. At that point, the Messiah enters the life of the believer. This ministry is recorded in John 3:3-7 and Titus 3:5-7.

The third ministry is **indwelling**. The ministry of indwelling is when the Holy Spirit is in the life of the believer, when the Holy Spirit indwells the believer just as the Messiah does in regeneration (I Cor. 3:16; 6:19; II Tim. 1:14).

The fourth ministry is the Spirit's ministry of **baptism**. When one believes, the Holy Spirit baptizes him into the Body of the Messiah (I Cor. 12:13; Eph. 4:4-6).

The fifth ministry is **sealing**. With this ministry, the believer is sealed into the Body of the Messiah so that he can never fall out; this is what provides his eternal security (II Cor. 1:21-22; Eph. 1:13-14; 4:30).

While the ministries of the Holy Spirit that pertain to one's salvation are once-and-for-all acts, the ministries that lead to his maturity are continuous. There are five such ministries:

1. The ministry of teaching spiritual truth (Jn. 16:12-16)
2. The ministry of guiding us (Rom. 8:14)
3. The ministry of assurance (Rom. 8:16)
4. The ministry of praying for us (Rom. 8:26)
5. The ministry of filling (Eph. 5:18)

These five ministries are continuous and repeated. They relate to spiritual maturity. Because they relate to spiritual maturity, they are the ones involved in the Spirit-filled life. This is especially true of the last one, so this discussion will move on to elaborate on the filling of the Holy Spirit.

The key passage that deals with the filling of the Holy Spirit is found in Ephesians 5:18:

And be not drunk with wine, wherein is [excess], *but be filled with the Spirit;*

It is this ministry which enables one to live a Spirit-filled life. By way of definition, to *be filled with the Spirit* means "to be Spirit-controlled." Just as someone who is filled with alcohol is controlled by the alcohol, the person who is filled with the Spirit is controlled by the Spirit. In order to allow the Spirit to control one's life in daily living, there must be the initial act of dedication of our lives to God which was already discussed at length.

The filling of the Spirit is a command because the Greek verb in Ephesians 5:18 is in the imperative form. Therefore, it is a requirement; believers are obligated by God to let the Spirit control their lives.

Furthermore, the filling is repeated. The imperative is in the present tense, which emphasizes repeated action. Filling should take place more than once. In the Book of Acts, for example, the disciples were filled first in Acts 2:4, filled again in Acts 4:8, and filled again in Acts 4:31. Stephen was filled by the Holy Spirit in Acts 6:5 and again in Acts 7:55. Paul was filled with the Spirit in Acts 9:17 and again in Acts 13:9. Filling is something that is repeated.

Another important characteristic of the filling is that someone else is doing it. In the Greek, the present imperative is in the passive voice, which means that someone else is the acting party. Obviously, it is the Holy Spirit who is doing the filling, and believers are submitting themselves to that control in their daily living.

The filling of the Spirit produces the likeness of the Messiah. This is seen in the rest of chapters five and six in the Book of Ephesians, where Paul spells out what is included in the Spirit-filled life: the likeness of the Messiah (Eph. 5:19—6:24).

There are certain conditions that support this ministry of the Holy Spirit. For example, there must be a dedicated life; one must be yielded to the Spirit's control. This involves the initial act of dedication (Rom. 12:1) and the continuous direction of one's life by the Spirit in daily living. A dedicated life is a prerequisite. Unless one has made that initial act of dedication, he cannot live the Spirit-filled life.

Another prerequisite is the undefeated life. What does this mean? An undefeated life means believers are living consistently with victory over sin in their daily experience. Ephesians 4:30 makes this a command:

And grieve not the Holy Spirit of God, in whom ye were sealed unto the day of redemption.

How can believers achieve this? The means is by responding to the *light* of the Word as it is continuously being understood (I Jn. 1:7).

The filling by the Spirit lastly requires a dependent life in which one leans on the work of the Spirit. Galatians 5:16 explains:

But I say, Walk by the Spirit, and ye shall not fulfil the lust of the flesh.

Obviously, these conditions involve our yieldedness and obedience to the Word of God.

The filling of the Spirit will produce several results.

1. It will bring the likeness of the Messiah in character because it will produce *the fruit of the Spirit* (Gal. 5:22-23).
2. It will produce worship and praise (Eph. 5:19-20). The believers will want to worship and praise God. Outwardly, they will be praising

Him by *speaking one to another in psalms and hymns and spiritual songs.* Inwardly, they will have an attitude of worship evidenced by *singing and making melody in our hearts.*

3. They will also experience a spirit of thankfulness: we will be *giving thanks always for all things* (Eph. 5:20).
4. A Spirit-filled life results in submissiveness (Eph. 5:21). This includes submissiveness one to another: wives to husbands, children to parents, employees to employers.
5. The last result is service, because a dedicated, Spirit-filled life results in the power to exercise one's spiritual gifts.

You can you know that you are living a Spirit-filled life by answering two questions.

First, have you made the initial dedication of Romans 12:1? If the answer is "yes," then second, as far as you know, are you yielded in every area of your life? If you can say, "yes" then you are living a Spirit-filled life.

However, always remember that tomorrow may bring some new tests!

3. Applications of the Lordship of the Messiah to Specific Areas

The third major section of the Lordship of the Messiah deals with the application. This section will be discussed in four specific areas: discipleship, giving, prayer, and marriage.

a. Discipleship

Discipleship can best be defined as a man's relationship to *Yeshua* the Messiah in three capacities: as a teacher, as a master, and as Lord.

There is clearly a progression in meaning of discipleship. The Bible portrays three levels of depth when it speaks about disciples. The word disciple itself means "learner."

The first level of discipleship refers to the merely curious ones. These are the ones mentioned in Matthew 5:1:

And seeing the multitudes, he went up into the mountain: and when he had sat down, his disciples came unto him:

Later, Matthew 13:2 states:

And there were gathered unto him great multitudes, so that he entered into a boat, and sat; and all the multitude stood on the beach.

A third passage dealing with this category is John 8:31:

Yeshua therefore said to those Jews that had believed him, If ye abide in my word, then are ye truly my disciples;

The people involved in these verses were the curious ones. At this point, they were merely learners, wanting to know who *Yeshua* was or who He claimed to be. They were no more than pupils in a school. For now, this was only an intellectual pursuit for them. The members of this group have not as yet responded one way or the other to the claims of *Yeshua*. The first level of discipleship includes merely the curious, the learner, the intellectual pursuer, and nothing more.

The second level of discipleship is for one who is convinced. This category is mentioned in John 2:11:

This beginning of his signs did Yeshua in Cana of Galilee, and manifested his glory; and his disciples believed on him.

When a person moves from being curious to being convinced, he moves from the first level of discipleship to the second level of discipleship. He believes the facts; he is convinced of the truth of the claim. In this example of John 2:11, the disciples were convinced of the truth of His claim to be the Messiah.

There is a third level of discipleship, the kind that actually involves the Lordship of the Messiah. This is the committed disciple. This is the one who has found out the facts, has believed and been saved, and is now committed and has dedicated his life to that truth. This kind of disciple is spoken of in Matthew 16:13-16:

> *[13]Now when Yeshua came into the parts of Caesarea Philippi, he asked his disciples, saying, Who do men say that the Son of man is? [14]And they said, Some say John the Baptist; some, Elijah; and others, Jeremiah, or one of the prophets. [15]He said unto them, But who say ye that I am? [16]And Simon Peter answered and said, You are the Messiah, the Son of the living God.*

Another passage on this same level of discipleship is John 6:66-68:

> *[66]Upon this many of his disciples went back, and walked no more with him. [67]Yeshua said therefore unto the twelve, Would ye also go away? [68]Simon Peter answered him, Lord, to whom shall we go? you have the words of eternal life.*

This passage actually describes two different groups of disciples: those who were merely convinced but would no longer follow Him, and, perhaps, these were the merely curious ones; but the others, the eleven, were third-level-disciples. They were committed; they were going to stick with *Yeshua* no matter what, because they knew He had *the words of eternal life.*

So there are three groups of disciples in the Scriptures: the merely curious ones or learners; the ones who are convinced but not committed to it; and the committed, dedicated believers. Those who have made the act of dedication and are living the Spirit-filled life fall into the category of the committed disciples. This is true discipleship. This is total commitment.

This is actually showing that the Messiah has become the Lord of one's life and that he is living the Spirit-filled life.

The demands of discipleship are spelled out in three passages. First is Matthew 16:24-26, which teaches that a disciple must say "no" to himself and *take up his cross*, which means he must be willing to be rejected even as *Yeshua* was rejected. The second passage is Luke 14:27, which also emphasizes that one must identify with the Messiah's rejection. Third, Luke 14:33 teaches that discipleship involves a total renunciation of what is first in one's life.

The demands of discipleship mean that believers are no longer in authority of their own lives. The Messiah is the Lord of their lives; He controls them, and they totally identify with Him. They have totally identified with His rejection, and they have totally renounced anything that might become the center of their lives besides Him.

Three passages spell out the means of becoming a disciple. The first verse, Matthew 11:29, points out two steps:

29Take my yoke upon you, and learn of me; for I am meek and lowly in heart: and ye shall find rest unto your souls.

The first step is, *Take my yoke*. "Taking His yoke" means to become His disciple. To become His disciple is to dedicate one's life once and for all. The second step is, *learn of me*. This is the means: learn of Him and become intimately acquainted with Him. One learns more about Him when He is the Lord of his life, and he is a disciple because he has made this total commitment.

The second passage, John 8:30-32, teaches that becoming a disciple means abiding in the teachings of the Messiah.

30As he spoke these things, many believed on him. 31Yeshua therefore said to those Jews that had believed him, If ye abide in my word, then are ye truly my disciples; 32and ye shall know the truth, and the truth shall make you free.

"Abiding in the Word" means, "to know His Word, to follow it, and obey it." Obedience is the key mark of a disciple.

In the third passage, Luke 14:28-30, *Yeshua* points out that becoming a disciple involves doing three things:

> *[28]For which of you, desiring to build a tower, does not first sit down and count the cost, whether he have wherewith to complete it? [29]Lest haply, when he has laid a foundation, and is not able to finish, all that behold begin to mock him, [30]saying, This man began to build, and was not able to finish.*

First, one must *count the cost* and not make a commitment rashly or foolishly. He should count the cost, realizing that once he makes this commitment, he has no guarantee of earthly comfort. He should count the cost of being a disciple because it is a terrible thing to make a commitment and not follow through. Second, having made a decision, there is to be no delay in following through. Once one has made a decision, he should fulfill it. Then, third, once having started on the road of discipleship, there must be no turning back, because that would be apostasy.

Another important fact of discipleship is found in the Great Commission of Matthew 28:18-20:

> *[18]And Yeshua came to them and spoke unto them, saying, All authority has been given unto me in heaven and on earth. [19]Go ye therefore, and make disciples of all the nations, baptizing them into the name of the Father and of the Son and of the Holy Spirit: [20]teaching them to observe all things whatsoever I commanded you: and lo, I am with you always, even unto the end of the world.*

The commission is not to evangelize, but to *make disciples*. In the Greek text, there is only one imperative, which is *make disciples*. The imperative is followed by three subordinate participial clauses: going, baptizing, and teaching. They spell out the three elements of making disciples: first, going means "evangelizing;" second, *baptizing* those who have believed; and third, *teaching* all things that God has commanded, because obedience is the mark of a disciple.

b. Giving

Giving is the second specific area of application of the Lordship of the Messiah. There are five passages of Scripture that teach on giving and its relationship to the Lordship of the Messiah.

(1) I John 3:17

But whoso has the world's goods, and beholds his brother in need, and shuts up his compassion from him, how does the love of God abide in him?

This first passage teaches that sharing materially with a fellow believer in need is evidence of spiritual life.

(2) II Corinthians 8:1-5

The second passage teaches that believers need to support the ministry and those in the ministry financially:

[1]Moreover, brethren, we make known to you the grace of God which has been given in the churches of Macedonia; [2]how that in much proof of affliction the abundance of their joy and their deep poverty abounded unto the riches of their liberality. [3]For according to their power, I bear witness, yea and beyond their power, they gave of their own accord, [4]beseeching us with much entreaty in regard of this grace and the fellowship in the ministering to the saints: [5]and this, not as we had hoped, but first they gave their own selves to the Lord, and to us through the will of God.

If a believer is not giving to the support of a ministry or ministries, he is not exercising the Lordship of the Messiah in this area.

(3) Galatians 6:6

The third passage teaches that the one who receives spiritual benefit from a teacher is obligated to share with that teacher in material benefits:

But let him that is taught in the word communicate unto him that teaches in all good things.

If a believer is being taught Scripture through a minister of a church, a Sunday School teacher, or a para-church ministry, and is not sharing the financial support of those from whom he is benefiting, he is not fulfilling the Lordship of the Messiah in this area of his life.

(4) I Corinthians 16:1-2

¹Now concerning the collection for the saints, as I gave order to the churches of Galatia, so also do ye. ²Upon the first day of the week let each one of you lay by him in store, as he may prosper, that no collections be made when I come.

There are four aspects of giving that can be learned from these verses. The first thing is that giving is required of all, for it states: *let each one of you.* Every believer is required to give.

Second, it teaches that giving should be proportionate: as God has prospered. There is no tithing for the New Testament believer. Tithing was only under the Law of Moses; it is not part of the law of the Messiah. However, if one is going to practice the Lordship of the Messiah, he must learn to practice Spirit-filled giving. Maybe sometimes only nine percent is possible, maybe at other times eleven percent, sometimes ninety percent. Actually, the Old Testament tithe was not ten percent; it was twenty-two percent if one were to add all three tithes together.

A believer's giving must be proportionate and as God has prospered him. Based on how God has prospered him, he needs to set aside a certain amount of money, be it ten, fifty, or ninety percent for the Lord's work.

The third thing this passage teaches is that giving should be in a separate account: *lay* [up] *in store.* The Greek word used here means "to store up" or "to treasure up." It is reflexive, meaning "to himself," and it is a private deposit, not some public depository like the church treasury. In other words, this is speaking of a private fund into which the Lord's money is placed and out of which one distributes to specific causes as he is led by the Spirit. Our family has two separate checking accounts. One is our operating account, from which we pay our food bills, car bills, mortgage, etc. We have a second checking account which we call "God's Account." We put the Lord's money into that account and what goes in there is never used to meet personal needs. Never! From then on, that is the Lord's money and, as we are led by the Spirit, we distribute this money to support various ministries.

There are various options by which one can fulfill it, but it must be a private deposit of some kind. "Laying up in store" does not rule out regular giving, like supporting the ministry of a congregation. Nor does it rule out making a pledge, because the Corinthians made a pledge, according to II Corinthians 8:10-11. There should always be an ever-ready supply of money available to give out as the Spirit directs, and the best way of accomplishing that is by way of a private deposit or separate account.

The fourth thing about giving is that it should be both periodic and organized: *the first day of the week.* The laying up in store should not be erratic, but on *the first day of the week.* From Paul's Jewish perspective, this was any time from sundown Saturday to sundown Sunday. On *the first day of the week,* one should sit down and see how God has prospered him financially. Then, based on the way He has prospered him financially, he is to take a portion of that amount, whatever percentage it might be, and put it away in some type of private deposit. Then, as the Spirit leads, he takes from this account and supports the Lord's work.

(5) Romans 15:25-27

Romans 15:25-27 points out that in missionary giving, one should follow the principle *to the Jew first* (Rom. 1:16):

²⁵but now, I say, I go unto Jerusalem, ministering unto the saints.
²⁶For it has been the good pleasure of Macedonia and Achaia to
make a certain contribution for the poor among the saints that are at
Jerusalem. ²⁷Yea, it has been their good pleasure; and their debtors
they are. For if the Gentiles have been made partakers of their
spiritual things, they owe it to them also to minister unto them in
carnal things.

As Gentiles become partakers of Jewish spiritual blessings, they are now
obligated to share material things with Jewish believers.

c. Prayer

The third specific area of application of the Lordship of the Messiah is
prayer. The best passage that explains this clearly is Luke 11:2-4:

²And he said unto them, When ye pray, say, Father, Hallowed be your
name. Your kingdom come. ³Give us day by day our daily bread. ⁴And
forgive us our sins; for we ourselves also forgive every one that is
indebted to us. And bring us not into temptation.

In these verses, *Yeshua* points out six things concerning the Lordship of the
Messiah in prayer.

1. All prayer is to be **addressed** to God the *Father*, not to the Son or
   the Holy Spirit.
2. Believers should **sanctify** God: *Hallowed be your name.*
3. They should pray for the **Kingdom Program**, which is the work of
   God. Since they know from prophecy that the Kingdom is coming,
   they can be sure that it will come. Therefore, they are to pray for the
   Kingdom to come. Part of the Kingdom Program is salvation, so
   they should be praying for the works of evangelism and missions.
4. They should be praying for their **personal needs**, emphasizing their
   dependence on God. This may seem petty, but it shows dependence

upon the Lordship of the Messiah. This is how the Lordship of the Messiah is applicable to their prayer life.

5. There should be **confession** of sin in order to restore the family relationship with God the Father. It is at this point, by means of confession, that the believers inspect the state of their dedication and the state of their filling to make sure that they are still on the track of a dedicated life, that they are still living the dedicated life.

6. Believers should be praying about **spiritual warfare**.

d. Marriage

The fourth specific area of application of the Lordship of the Messiah is marriage. Marriage, perhaps more than anything else, is the imitation of the Lordship of the Messiah. Just as the husband is the lord of the wife, even so the Messiah should be the Lord of the believer. Ephesians 5:22-23 elaborates on this relationship:

²²Wives, be in subjection unto your own husbands, as unto the Lord. ²³For the husband is the head of the wife, as Christ also is the head of the church, being himself the saviour of the body.

In applying the Lordship of *Yeshua* to marriage, five things can be pointed out based upon this passage.

1. The wife is to surrender to the lordship of the husband to the extent that she would submit to the Lordship of the Messiah.

2. An unsubmissive wife is in rebellion against the Lordship of the Messiah. If a wife is in rebellion against her husband, she is rebelling against God. It is that simple.

3. The reason this submission should be there is because of the love of the Messiah.

4. The husband is obligated to love his wife into subjection, not force her into subjection. Forcing a wife into subjection by mistreating her, verbally or physically, is rebellion against the Lordship of the Messiah. An abusive husband is not in submission to Messiah's

Lordship. It is as simple as that. A husband who is not loving his wife is not loving God either.

5. A husband is to do his best to bring his wife to perfection in the area of her gifts and her talents.

Chapter VI – Conclusion

Salvation is by grace through faith totally apart from works. It is a free gift received by faith. The only requirement is to believe the gospel that *Yeshua* died for one's sins, was buried (the evidence of His death), and rose again (I Corinthians 15:1-4). That alone must be believed for salvation. As soon as any "plus" is added, it will pervert the gospel. Different people have added a plus such as baptism, repentance (defined as feeling sorry for one's sins), confession, or other things which corrupt the gospel and hide what it is one must believe to be saved.

A major reason for confusion is a lack of understanding the difference between salvation and discipleship. Salvation is a free gift given to those who believe the gospel. Once one believes, he has eternal life and has it forever. Discipleship requires commitment of one's life and body to be used for and by the Lord.

In Romans 1-11, Paul provided a detailed teaching on the theology of God's righteousness. He showed how all humanity, the pagan Gentile world, the cultured Gentile world, and the Jewish world have all fallen short of the righteousness of God. Thus, God took the initiative and provided salvation for all in three time zones: justification, the past aspect of our salvation; sanctification, the present aspect of our salvation; and glorification, the future aspect of our salvation. So, based on all that God has done for the believer, Paul goes on to encourage the believer to present his body a living sacrifice for the Lord's use (Rom. 12:1-2). This one act of commitment begins the road to discipleship where the believer moves from immaturity to maturity and from milk to meat. Those who make such a commitment and remain faithful to it are promised a life of fellowship in this age and great rewards in the age to come.

Bibliography

Bauer, Walter, F. Wilbur Gingrich, Frederick W. Danker, and Walter Bauer. *A Greek-English Lexicon of the New Testament and Other Early Christian Literature: A Translation and Adaptation of the Fourth Revised and Augmented Edition of Walter Bauer's Griechisch-Deutsches Wörterbuch zu den Schriften des Neuen Testaments und der übrigen urchristlichen Literatur.* Chicago: University of Chicago Press, 1979

Grimm, Carl Ludwig Wilibald, Joseph Henry Thayer, and Christian Gottlob Wilke. *Greek-English Lexicon of the New Testament; Being Grimm's Wilke's Clavis Novi Testamenti.* Grand Rapids: Zondervan Pub. House, 1970

Harrison, Everett F. & John R. Stott, "Must Christ Be Lord To Be Savior?" *Eternity* 10(9):13-18, 36-7, 48, September. 1959

Hendriksen, William. *Exposition of Galatians.* Grand Rapids, Michigan: Baker Book House, 1968

Johnson Jr, S. Lewis. Paul and 'The Israel of God': An Exegetical and Eschatological Case-Study. *The Master's Seminary Journal 20(1):*41-55 Spring 2009

MacArthur, John. *The Parables of the Kingdom.* Chicago: Moody Press, 1985

Packer, J. I. *Evangelism & the Sovereignty of God.* Downers Grove, IL: Intervarsity Press, 1961

Pink, Arthur Walkington. *Studies on Saving Faith.* Granbury, TX: PBM Desktop Publications, 2005

Robinson, Donald WB. "The distinction between Jewish and Gentile believers in Galatians." *Australian Biblical Review 13* (1965)

Scripture Index

CPSIA information can be obtained
at www.ICGtesting.com
Printed in the USA
FSOW02n1341111215
14030FS